MISSISSIPPI ESCAPADE

The *Morning Star* leaving St. Louis, Missouri, for St. Paul, Minnesota, in 1895.

MISSISSIPPI ESCAPADE

Reliving the Grand Excursion of 1854

PAUL CLIFFORD LARSON *and* PAMELA ALLEN LARSON

Afton Historical Society Press
Afton, Minnesota

Publication of

MISSISSIPPI ESCAPADE

was made possible by
a generous donation from

Target, Marshall Field's,
and Mervyn's

with support from the

Target Foundation.

Additional funding was provided by the

Harlan Boss Foundation
for the Arts

and

Dick and Nancy Nicholson.

These donors are also placing copies
of this book in Minnesota classrooms as
part of Afton Historical Society Press's
Books for Schools Program.

This book is dedicated to our parents, Clifford and Adda Mary Larson and Gilbert and Enid Allen, who introduced us to the joy of discovering new places.   P. C.L. and P. A.L.

Cover: St Paul, oil painting by S. Holmes Andrews, 1855 (Minnesota Historical Society).

Edited by Michele Hodgson
Designed by Mary Susan Oleson
Printed by Pettit Network, Inc.

Library of Congress Cataloging-in-Publication Data

Larson, Paul Clifford.
Mississippi Escapade : Reliving the Grand Excursion of 1854 / Paul Clifford Larson and Pamela Allen Larson—1st ed.
p. cm.
ISBN 1-890434-64-7 (pbk. : alk. paper)
1. Mississippi River—Description and travel—Juvenile literature.
2. Mississippi River Valley—Description and travel—Juvenile literature.
3. Mississippi River Valley—History—1803-1865—Juvenile literature.
I. Larson, Pamela Allen. II. Title.

F353.L37 2004
977—dc   222003022369
Printed in China

Afton Historical Society Press publishes
exceptional books on regional subjects.

W. Duncan MacMillan   Patricia Condon Johnston
President   Publisher

Contents

Preface 6

Note to Educators and Parents 10

1   BEFORE THE GRAND EXCURSION   11

2   FROM RAILS TO RIVER   25

3   STEAMBOATS AND SMOKESTACKS   41

4   THE EAGLE AND THE INDIAN   59

5   CITIES AND SPECTACLE   77

6   LAKE PEPIN AND BEYOND   93

7   THE EDGE OF CIVILIZATION   107

More River Activities 122

River Resources 124

Illustration Credits 128

Preface

Traveling on the Upper Mississippi River has always been a grand adventure. Since the first steamboat reached Fort Snelling in 1823, the scenic wonders of the stretch of river between Illinois and Minnesota have been justly celebrated by vacationers, writers, artists, scientific observers, and town promoters. Even the most jaded nineteenth-century New England visitor, fresh from his luxuriously appointed "wilderness" vacation in New York's Adirondack Mountains, could not help but be awed by the river's unfolding vistas of tree-filled islands, towering bluffs, and westward-stretching prairies.

Until the middle of the nineteenth century, little had changed the winding course of the upper river valley since the last glaciers retreated 12,000 years before. The landscapes that had greeted the Archaic Indians in their dugout canoes were the same ones that urbane eastern visitors saw from their floating palaces.

But as white settlement spread along either shore of the Mississippi, it brought with it changes more radical to the shape and course of the river than those wrought by thousands of years of rushing wind and water. The pivotal decade was the 1850s, and its central event the Grand Excursion of 1854. A railroad line—the first to reach the Mississippi—had been completed from the Atlantic coast to Rock Island, Illinois, in February of that year. More than 1,000 curious excursionists—most of them invited by the Chicago and Rock Island Railroad—flocked to the city's steamboat landing early in June, ready to embark for Minnesota Territory on what for many would be the adventure of their lives. Journalists were the dominant group, but the excursionists also included large contingents of scientists from Yale and public figures and ministers from East Coast cities, St. Louis, and Chicago. All would steam north to St. Paul, accomplishing the trip in two-and-a-half days.

MISSISSIPPI ESCAPADE tells the story of the Grand Excursion. But the main focus of the book is not the travelers, or even their particular adventure. The ruling subject is the mighty river itself and the humans who settled along the stretch of shoreline that the excursionists steamed by.

The Grand Excursion of 1854 is a perfect starting place for a virtual tour of the modern Mississippi, as well as for the excursion's reenactment in 2004. The landscapes described by the excursionists are still the marvel they were 150 years ago. Moreover, the 1854 travelers saw in their infancy the villages that would evolve into the large urban centers along the river today. The many towns created by mining interests and other speculative efforts were already passing in 1854; communities that survived were, by and large, on their way to lasting success. Rock Island, Illinois, and Davenport, Iowa, were growing their first clusters of "permanent" (that is, masonry) downtown buildings. Dubuque, Iowa, was settling in as a major supply center for the Upper Mississippi and lands to the west. Winona, Minnesota, and La Crosse, Wisconsin, were barely three years old but showing early promise. While serving as the Minnesota territorial capital, St. Paul had that spring been incorporated as a city.

The experiences of the Grand Excursionists of 1854 took place against a historic backdrop that had already brought western lands, and the Mississippi River in particular, before the eyes and imaginations of the East.

Steamboat (Mississippi) by E. A. Banks, ca. 1870.

Grand tours of the expanding American nation were rapidly coming into vogue, and one of the most popular was a steamboat trip north from New Orleans or St. Louis. Vast painted panoramas, based on artistic pilgrimages along the river in the 1840s, rolled on stage between eight-foot scrolls, entertaining throngs in England and Germany as well as America. During the year of the Grand Excursion one of the most famous panorama painters, Henry Lewis, was preparing dozens of Mississippi River scenes for publication. Other notable artists, George Catlin and Seth Eastman foremost among them, had devoted a decade and more to rendering images of American Indian life in the Central Plains, many of them capturing the physical character of the land they occupied. Illustrated articles celebrating the river's wild beauty, Indian lore, and makeshift white settlements appeared in popular magazines such as *Harper's Monthly*. A lavish subscription volume called *The United States, Illustrated,* issued serially between 1853 and 1855, prominently featured the Upper Mississippi. Thus the Grand Excursion simply rode the wake of a rising tide of interest in the river and its possibilities for settlement.

Traveller's Guide through the United States and Canada by Wellington Williams, 1851.

As modern writers and readers, without eastern editors or transportation officials breathing down our necks, we have paid much more attention to the river's lesser communities and landmarks than the excursionists did. Local sites, some of them barely publicized beyond county boundaries, are what provide variety and texture along the river of the twenty-first century. They are as much a part of its history and its future as the larger urban centers.

SCORES OF INDIVIDUALS, institutions, and city agencies enriched our knowledge and our experience as we returned again and again to the Great River Road to observe, research, and take photographs for MISSISSIPPI ESCAPADE. We are especially grateful to numerous townspeople who provided an abundance of new leads, information, and, above all, stories about the river. Ten were particularly generous with their time: Mary Beeler of the Pierce County Historical Association River Bluffs History Center in Bay City, Wisconsin; restaurateur Daryll Eggers of Potter's Mill in Bellevue, Iowa; artist David Geister of St. Paul, Minnesota, and Prescott, Wisconsin; wood-carver M. H. Langseth of Minneiska, Minnesota; John Malcom of

Rivertown Fine Books in McGregor, Iowa; educator Theresa McHenry of La Crosse, Wisconsin; antiquarian Bill Marshall of Wyalusing, Wisconsin; history buffs Clyde and Debbie Overturff of Dubuque, Iowa; and innkeeper LaVerne Waldbusser of Port Byron, Illinois.

For most of the last century, much of the finest historical work on lesser Mississippi River towns has been done by local historians such as Barbara Anderson-Sannes of Alma, Wisconsin; the late Walter W. Jacobs of Guttenberg, Iowa; Dorothy Eaton Ahlgren and Mary Cotter Beeler of Prescott, Wisconsin; and Roald Tweet of the Quad Cities, to name a particularly noteworthy handful. Every river town has its "river rats," each of them a fount of anecdotes and information, mostly of the variety that should be true whether it is or not. Many Web sites have also provided important leads; the broader ranging and factually more reliable of these are listed among the resources beginning on page 124. We have also drawn liberally from the visual resources of the Minnesota Historical Society and the State Historical Society of Wisconsin. The University of Minnesota Libraries were gracious enough to allow copy photography of a number of rare maps and wood engravings.

View on the Upper Mississippi, Beautiful River Bluffs by George Catlin, 1835–1836.

Finally, we owe a debt of gratitude to Afton Historical Society Press for once again tackling a regional project with a commitment both to the subject at hand and to the audience that MISSISSIPPI ESCAPADE is intended to stimulate, to inform, and along the way, to entertain. The themes of this book are meant to be accessible to upper elementary schoolchildren and their families, but we believe they are of equal interest to anyone with a bit of the river in their blood.

Paul Clifford Larson, REGIONAL HISTORIAN
Pamela Allen Larson, TEACHER

Note to Educators and Parents

The Upper Mississippi River Valley offers a wealth of educational opportunities for classrooms as well as recreational activities for families. The activities suggested throughout MISSISSIPPI ESCAPADE are only a fraction of what the river and its communities have to offer. Use them as a jumping-off place for further river exploration.

Many of the activities can be adapted to different topics throughout the book. They are intended for young people to follow on their own or for teachers to extend for classroom use. On pages 122 and 123 are additional activities that relate to the Mississippi River experience as a whole rather than to any particular segment. All of them integrate artistic activity into learning more about the river. They are also a good deal of fun.

Many learning resources are listed within the chapter activities. A more complete list can be found beginning on page 124. All provide links to further adventures. Some Web sites and popularly written books in the resource list should be used with caution; a good deal of Mississippi lore, including tales of the Grand Excursion of 1854, tends to be repeated over time with little check on its truth or falsity.

The Mississippi River continues to draw Americans of every background to its banks to sketch, paint, write, sing, play, and work. Curiosity brought the Grand Excursionists to see the river's wilderness and its storied bluffs, infant white settlements, and passing Indian culture. With this book as a guide, let the curiosity and imagination of your children and pupils lead them (and you) on their own river adventure!

Sunrise over the Mississippi from Pike's Peak, Iowa.

Paul and Pamela Larson

1

BEFORE THE GRAND EXCURSION

The Early Mississippi

In the description of American scenery the Mississippi river, as of royal right, claims a leading place. It is our Nile, our mythic stream.

R. E. Garczynski
Picturesque America, 1874

Upper Mississippi River by Henry Lewis, 1855.

*L*ong before people existed in North America, a great river at its center flowed south to the sea. But in those ancient times that river, first known as the Father of Waters, was much shorter than it is now. Seven hundred thousand years ago, the mighty Mississippi sprang from rocks, not in northern Minnesota, but in the southeastern part of the state where St. Paul now stands.

Not until the first Ice Age ended did the upper river as we know it begin to form. Beginning 12,000 years ago, as the glaciers melted and flowed south, they formed deep channels of water. One channel wound its way from the ancient Mississippi source to a lake 500 miles upstream—a lake now called Itasca. As the melting ice carved the old riverbed south of St. Paul, it created wide valleys and towering bluffs that transformed the Upper Mississippi River into one of the scenic wonders of the American continent.

Woodland culture mound builders at work.

Steamboat captains and pilots of the nineteenth century knew that the Upper Mississippi actually stretched hundreds of miles into northern Minnesota. But St. Paul was as far as their boats could go. The Falls of St. Anthony a few miles north were impassable, and above them the river became too narrow and treacherous for large watercraft. So what the captains and their passengers knew as the Upper Mississippi—the stretch between Rock Island, Illinois, and St. Paul—was just that area where nature had done its most dramatic work.

This was the part of the river toured by the Grand Excursion of 1854. In February of that year, the Chicago and Rock Island Railroad had completed the last link of rail connecting the Atlantic seaboard to the Mississippi River. In celebration, the railroad invited more than 1,000 passengers to travel at its expense from their homes on the East Coast (as well as Ohio, Illinois, and Missouri) to Rock Island. From there they embarked on a trip up the Mississippi River to St. Paul.

Steamboat landings and fledging cities dotted the shores, but the river journey brought the excursionists as close to pure wilderness as most of them would ever experience.

Indians still lived along the Grand Excursion's route, but their villages were fast disappearing. The Indians were distant descendants of the First People of the American continent, who appeared along the lakes and rivers that remained behind at the end of the last Ice Age. These First People are known as Paleo-Indians. They are also called Big Game Hunters, for they roamed the marshes and woodlands for woolly mammoths, caribou, and the giant beaver. The gradual drying and warming of the land drove these huge animals to extinction.

When a moister climate returned to the Upper Mississippi Valley about 8,000 years ago, a new human culture arose, one that hunted and fished, and gathered nuts along the river. These people are called Archaic Indians, also known as Hunters and Gatherers. They established a vast trading network up and down the Mississippi and its tributaries. Spear points and other traces of their seasonal camps are the oldest human artifacts to be found near the Mississippi River.

The most ancient evidence of human culture the Grand Excursionists of 1854 saw belonged to the Woodland Indians, who appeared in the Upper Mississippi River Valley 2,000 years ago. Their cities and villages had vanished many centuries before, but the Woodland Indians left behind great piles of earth and artifact, typically arranged into loose clusters. These were their burial mounds, in which they placed not only their dead but also sacred objects. Their most unusual earthworks, called effigy mounds, are shaped like animals and appear along ridges and bluffs lining the Upper Mississippi shores, particularly in Wisconsin and Iowa.

Bluffs below St. Paul by Herrmann Meyer, 1853–1855.

VISIONING THE RIVER

Visit a Mississippi River bluff or look at a picture of one (above and throughout the book). Look across the river to the opposite shore. Imagine the space between filled with water. How wide would it be? How deep? Then look at the bluff itself, especially the places where rocks protrude. How do you think centuries of wind and rain have changed the bluff? Do you see changes made by humans?

*Indians Spearing Fish 3 Miles below Fort Snelling
by Seth Eastman, 1846–1848.*

THE FIRST PEOPLE

Create a timeline of the river's peoples, starting with the Paleo-Indians. Include details about where and how they lived. Learn more about them at a museum, at a library, and on the Internet. Had the Grand Excursionists heard about them? Add explorers, settlers, and other people to the timeline as you learn about them.

According to living Indians and white settlers, the First People on the Upper Mississippi were the Oneotas, whose villages began to appear about 1,000 years ago. The Oneota were part of a much larger culture that was centered on the Mississippi River and its tributaries. At their peak, these Mississippian cultures were the most populous native societies in North America. Oneotas were also the first to practice large-scale agriculture along the upper river, raising corn, beans, and squash. They hunted bison with bows and arrows, just like nineteenth-century Indians occupying the vast plains west of the Mississippi. Oneota villages and mounds abounded near Red Wing, Minnesota, and La Crosse, Wisconsin, but the people had migrated westward 200 years before the Grand Excursion. French trappers called them the Ioway, which is how the state of Iowa got its name.

In the early decades of the nineteenth century, westward expansion of white settlement brought unrest to the already changing pattern of native Upper Mississippi River occupation. The Ojibwe (now often called Anishinaabe), whose roots were on the Atlantic coast, had been migrating westward for at least two centuries. When they reached what is now Wisconsin, they came in conflict with the Dakota and Ho-Chunk peoples. These were the Indian nations called Sioux and Winnebago by the French. By the turn of the nineteenth century the Ojibwe and Dakota had become fixed enemies. One reason white people built so many forts on the Upper Mississippi, such as Fort Snelling near St. Paul, was to ensure that Indian conflicts would not enlarge into wars that might endanger trappers, traders, and pioneers.

As early as 1804, the Sac (or Sauk) Indians of Illinois had assigned to the U.S. government the land they occupied on the east bank of the river. But their warrior chief, Ma-ka-tai-me-she-kia-kiak (known among whites as Black Hawk), had not agreed to the treaty. Black Hawk's return to his people's ancestral farmlands in 1832 brought about the Black Hawk War. The war and the Sacs themselves were but a part of Mississippi lore by 1854, but many sites along the river kept alive the memory of Black Hawk, the desperation of his people, and their final, violent expulsion from the east side of the Mississippi.

In 1837, the Ho-Chunk (Winnebago) Indians of Wisconsin were also pushed west of the Mississippi. Eleven years after that they were removed from Iowa to Long Prairie in the central part of what would become Minnesota Territory. A traveler on the river in the 1840s, Charles Lanman, noted that the Winnebagos were "once almost as numerous as the leaves upon the trees. . . . They were a race of brave men and beautiful women, but now they prowl among their native hills a brotherhood of vagabonds."

Finally, a series of treaties culminating in the Traverse de Sioux in 1851 officially moved the Dakotas from the west bank of the river and onto reservations in western Minnesota Territory. Many Dakota villages on the

CREATING MOUNDS

Some Indians created their burial mounds in the shape of animals by using tools handmade from clam shells, bone, and wood. To make a miniature mound of your own, shape a patch of earth like an animal. Try using something you find in nature as your digging tool. (Be sure to ask permission from an adult before starting to dig.) Keep track of how long it takes you to finish. Imagine how long it took the Mississippians to create their large mounds.

A restored Oneota bowl at Effigy Mounds National Monument Museum.

Black Hawk in Ceremonial Dress by Charles B. King, 1837.

Mississippi remained, particularly in the area of Minnesota between Red Wing and Hastings. Ojibwe and Winnebago lodges and camps also continued to survive on the Wisconsin side of the river. But these were a small remnant of the Indian peoples who had ranged freely over the river valley before the arrival of white settlers.

What the Grand Excursionists saw were the last traces of independent Indian society, and their contacts with the Indians were fleeting. Like many tourists before and after 1854, they saw just enough to fuel whatever romantic notions or prejudices about Indians they already possessed, but not enough to understand what a rich and complex civilization was threatened with extinction.

SPEAKING SAC

His people knew Chief Black Hawk as "Ma-ka-tai-me-she-kia-kiak." Try to pronounce it. Through books and the Internet, learn more about Black Hawk. Find Web sites, using the search words "Black Hawk" and "Sac" or "Sauk." How many different stories about him can you find? How do the stories differ from each other?

USING THE RIVER

Before the first steamboat arrived on the Mississippi, human use of the river had little effect on it or its environment. The Upper Mississippi flowed through a maze of meandering channels, its banks and course shifting from year to year and season to season as the weather and the wind dictated. Indians, explorers, fur trappers, and soldiers all traveled by canoe, with nothing but paddles to steer and propel them.

Early commercial watercraft were equally accepting of the river and its irregularities and dangers. In the 1750s, just as the French and the British were going to war over control of the West, French fur trappers introduced the keelboat on the Mississippi. As a means of

Sioux Encampment, Upper Mississippi by F. Jackson, 1857.

Scenery of the Upper Mississippi, An Indian Village, ca. 1870.

DEPICTING THE AMERICAN INDIAN

Artists who drew and painted Indian villages along the Upper Mississippi often added details to "flesh out," or embellish, the scene. The artist who painted the watercolor at the top left based it on his direct observations made during a trip in 1848. About two decades later, the famous art publishers Currier and Ives made a print of the same scene (see bottom left). What changes did Currier and Ives make? Notice the background and the foliage in the print as well as the people. Why do you think the publishers added those changes?

The Keel-Boat by I. M. L., 1855.

commercial transport, keelboats were a great improvement on even the largest and stablest of canoes. They could carry up to 30,000 pounds of freight, yet their draft (a term for how deep a boat sits in the water) was only two feet. Some keelboats were as long as eighty feet, requiring a crew of ten men. One sang out commands from atop the cabin where the goods were stowed, one stood at the rear with a sweep (a kind of rudder) in hand to steer the boat, and the remaining eight pushed the boat forward with long poles. Keelboats did not dominate transportation on the Mississippi River until the beginning of the nineteenth century, and by then the steamboat had already been invented. By the time of the Grand Excursion, the keelboat was already becoming a relic. However, eastern artists continued to feature them prominently in their pictures of the Mississippi River for the remainder of the 1800s. Keelboats were part of the romance of the West.

Equally passive in their use of the river were giant rafts made of logs. From their introduction in the 1830s until the early 1870s, the rafts were propelled and steered

RAFTING ON THE MISSISSIPPI

Create a mini log raft by arranging four toothpicks in a square with glue. Fill in the square with other toothpicks lined up in the same direction. That makes one raft square. Make more raft squares, then arrange them in a long line. That makes one string of rafts. Place more strings of the same length side by side. That is how the largest log rafts were made. For a virtual ride on a log raft, visit the River Museum in Dubuque, Iowa.

Raft of logs and lumber transported by steamboats from Stillwater, Minnesota, to Dubuque, Iowa, 1904.

without the use of boats. Simply rigged sails sometimes enlisted the help of the wind, but like the keelboats the rafts depended on man power. Sometimes they were pulled along the river's shore with ropes, sometimes poled off the river bottom like the keelboats, sometimes propelled by the river's current and steered by multiple long oars. Once the technique had been developed for lashing logs into square sections, and then into long rows, or "strings," rafts were often permitted to float down-river without human guidance. Even after the grand "river palace" steamboats appeared, the great size and unwieldiness of rafts gave them absolute right of way.

Canoes, keelboats, and rafts needed no fuel from the shore. Their crews also had little means of transforming the treacherous rapids or shifting sandbars. These were simply accepted as hazards of river travel. Steamboats changed all of this forever. The demands they made on the river and its environment marked the beginning of a concerted attempt to harness the river for human

Snags by I. M. L, 1855.

purposes. In the process, steamboating put into motion a cycle of human activity that would change the Mississippi more in 100 years than nature had altered it in 10,000.

The first part of the river environment to show the effects of steamboat traffic was the dense growth of trees along the shore. Early steamboats consisted of little more than a boiler and a shack perched on a raft, but they soon evolved into floating hotels with an endless appetite for wood.

Riverboats of Grand Excursion times typically stopped two or three times a day to pick up fuel in the form of logs cut into pieces known as cordwood. This was called "wooding up." The average daily consumption of wood for a single steamboat was twenty cords, which would be a pile four feet deep, four feet high, and 160 feet long. (Imagine a large living room—or a small classroom—sixteen by twenty feet, filled with wood from floor to ceiling. That is how much fuel a steamboat burned in twenty-four hours.) Within decades, steamboat landings and other refueling places along the river became barren of large trees for a great distance in all directions. Logs soon had to be transported to the "wooding up" places via wagon. By 1874, wood had become so hard to come by that coal became the fuel of choice.

Steamboats were equally taxing on the character of the river. They lay much deeper in the water than keelboats and rafts. That made them more vulnerable to obstacles in the river such as fallen tree branches, reefs, and

Starting a woodpile at the foot of Lake Pepin, 1847.

ARE YOU UP TO WOODING UP?

The distance traveled by the Grand Excursion was 400 miles one way. If the fleet traveled eight miles an hour, how long would it have taken to reach St. Paul if the boats had made no stops? Assuming each boat burned twenty cords of wood every twenty-four hours, how many cords did the entire fleet consume?

Steam Shovel dredging a channel at Sabula, Iowa, ca. 1915.

TAMING THE RIVER

Humorist and riverboat pilot Mark Twain said, "The Mississippi River will always have its own way; no engineering skill can persuade it to do otherwise." Many people who live on the river today say much the same thing. What do they mean by that? Think of examples where the river has overcome human attempts to control it. Can people ever become masters of the river? Why or why not?

submerged rocks. The first of these obstacles to be tackled by steamboaters were limbs from fallen trees, called snags. Specially designed snag boats appeared on the Upper Mississippi as early as 1829. They were unlike anything known elsewhere in the world. The boats ran full steam into snags to tear them loose. The crew then hoisted the branches on deck and broke them apart. Clearing the snags, called "pulling the river's teeth," led to a dramatic drop in shipping times and costs. Knowing that the river was free of snags also allowed night travelers, such as the Grand Excursionists were much of the time, to eat and dance under the stars without fear of their boat colliding with unseen dangers.

The job of clearing the geological barriers to navigation fell to a branch of the federal government, the U.S. Army Corps of Engineers. When it was created shortly after the American Revolution, the Army Corps of Engineers had the important task of exploring, surveying, and mapping western rivers. The object of its work was to establish both military outposts and commercial water routes.

Once commercial routes had been established, the Army Corps of Engineers' mission began to change. With the rise of large-scale commercial river use, it became the corps' responsibility not just to engineer building along the river, but to engineer the river itself. In the years before the Grand Excursion, that involved little more than finding sites for lumber and flour mills along the embankment at the Falls of St. Anthony, removing snags, and dredging a channel through sandbars and reefs just above Rock Island, Illinois.

In the late 1860s, after the Civil War was over, the Army Corps of Engineers became increasingly engaged in regulating bridge construction, dredging a deep and constant channel for navigation, and eventually creating a lock and dam system along the length of the river as far as St. Louis, Missouri. By the end of the 1930s, completion of the lock and dam system had transformed the Mississippi from a continuously flowing, shifting, winding stream to a

"stairway of water." The twenty-eight long stretches of open water above and below locks are known as pools, with the locks themselves providing a means of stepping up or down from one pool to the next.

During the rapid rise in steamboat traffic on the Mississippi, the people who used the river changed even more than the river itself. By the 1850s, explorers, fur trappers, and other rough-hewn frontiersmen had given way to a cross section of American society. Leading the way were those who traveled entirely for pleasure. Like

Lock and Dam 10 at Guttenberg, Iowa, viewed from a Grand Excursion—era warehouse.

Sunday Afternoon on the Levee in Winona, Minnesota by S. J. Durran, 1895.

the hotels and public squares and parks of cities, steamboats became places for the wealthy and the educated to socialize, to give impromptu lectures, to hold dances and political discussions, and to show off the latest fashions. Several well-traveled passengers aboard the Grand Excursion were pleasantly astonished at the politeness of the crew, the elegance of the accommodations, and the elaborateness of the meals so far removed from the East Coast. They should not have been. The Mississippi steamboat offered a remarkable view on the western wilderness, but the experience of that view was guided and shaped by the citified tastes and fancies of the East.

2

Launching the Grand Excursion

Davenport and Rock Island City by Henry Lewis, 1855.

Our eastern friends, who have not seen the evidence with their own eyes, can have no possible conception of the rapid settlement of this western country.

James F. Babcock
Grand Excursion reporter

The Grand Excursion of June 1854 began at a thousand easterners' doorsteps. For the first leg of their trip, the Chicago and Rock Island Railroad had promised the passengers delivery from their homes to the nearest railroad station, then a ride by train to Chicago. Most of the travelers came from Connecticut or New York, but nearly all of the states from Massachusetts to Illinois were represented.

Many travelers started their trip in late May to visit relatives or tourist sites along the way. Niagara Falls in western New York, already one of the most famous scenic spots in America, was a favorite stop. But few took this first stage of the trip to be part of the adventure. The train ride to Chicago was just a way to gather passengers into the city's largest hotels so that the real excursion could begin. Many leading citizens of Chicago—including ministers, public figures, and wealthy industrialists—joined the travelers. They all packed into two specially reserved trains bound for Rock Island.

Looking out the windows of the train cars en route to

The Mississippi from Rock Island, Illinois, to Le Claire, Iowa.

Rock Island was the first experience most of the excursionists had of the beginnings of the Far West. Chicago was the last outpost of white settlement that easterners knew much about. Everything west of that they regarded as wilderness. Towns neatly laid out with beautiful homes, stately churches, and business blocks took them by surprise. And they hadn't even reached the Mississippi River yet.

ROCK ISLAND

In 1854, Rock Island was still a quiet place. People buying and selling land were everywhere, but the settlement still had much of its beautiful natural setting. More than one traveler of the period wrote about it as a pretty town. But on June 5, Rock Island was a party town.

Nearly 1,000 sightseers poured from the two Grand Excursion trains from Chicago. They were joined by a horde of local citizens and travelers who came up the river from St. Louis. Though uninvited, they had heard about the excursion and wanted to join in. The easterners rushed to the riverbank for their first look at the Mississippi. This would mark the beginning of the climactic stage of their adventure, a passage up the great river to St. Paul.

Ticket for the Grand Excursion of 1854.

Rock Island City by Herrmann J. Meyer, 1853–1855.

REPORTING THE GRAND EXCURSION

Imagine that you are a newspaper reporter aboard the Grand Excursion of 1854. Write an article describing an event, a town, or the landscape that would give readers back East a vivid idea of what the Upper Mississippi River looked like back then. Will you describe the river as too wild a place to live or will you call it a good place to settle? Use the book's pictures as well as the text to get descriptive details to include in your article.

1892 statue of Black Hawk at Hauberg Indian Museum, Rock Island.

BLACK HAWK TODAY

Even 167 years after his death, Black Hawk remains one of the most memorable figures of Mississippi River history. Using the Internet and the library, find places, events, and things named after the great Sac leader. Organize the information into a chart.

Rock Island is a perfect place to begin traveling back in time as well, for the town captures the entire human history of the Upper Mississippi. Paleo-Indians camped above its shore as many as 12,000 years ago, and the remains of great burial mounds showed that the Mississippian people had lived there as well. In more recent times, toward the beginning of the eighteenth century, the Sac (or Sauk) people had located their capital on the riverbank. Saukenuk, as it was called, was one of the largest Indian centers in North America.

Saukenuk was laid out in a way that even a New Englander could have appreciated, with streets and blocks divided into lots. Long bark-covered log houses surrounded a central square. According to Sac chief Black Hawk, "We always had plenty. Our children never cried from hunger; neither were our people in want."

For a century the Sac dominated much of the Upper Mississippi River trade. They raised corn on the eastern side and enjoyed friendly relations with fur trappers and traders. But by the early 1820s, when steamboats first ventured north of St. Louis, white settlement had already pushed the Sac Indians and their allies, the Mesquakie (also known as Fox), to the western side of the river. The unhappy ending of these times took place farther up the river, in Wisconsin lands far from their ancestral home. But in Rock Island, the memory of the region's native cultures is kept alive by Hauberg Indian Museum, the centerpiece of the Black Hawk State Historic Site.

The present city of Rock Island sits on the Illinois shore, but a nearby island actually gave the city its name and was the first place occupied by white settlers. After the War of 1812, U.S. soldiers came to the island to build Fort Armstrong to keep British soldiers and traders off the Upper Mississippi. After the fort was completed in 1816, George Davenport came upriver to run a supply post for the army. Davenport established trading posts up and down the river and soon became an influential and wealthy man, respected by settlers and native peoples alike. He built a stone mansion in 1834 on the island not far from the fort. The Colonel Davenport House remains a romantic reminder of a time when the island was largely forest and there were no cities on either shore.

Fort Armstrong outlived its usefulness in the 1830s and was replaced by a military arms depot. After the Civil War, the depot grew into a great weapons manufacturing plant and supply depot for the U.S. army. Between 1866 and 1893 ten monumental stone buildings arose. Still in use by the army, they have been declared a National Historic Landmark. The buildings also gave their name to the land they occupy: Arsenal Island.

When the city of Rock Island was platted (divided into lots) in 1835, Davenport would have been the obvious choice for a name. Robbers had just killed the old trader at his island home, so naming the town after him would have been a fitting memorial. But George Davenport's staunch defense of Indian rights had infuriated an Illinois

Fort Armstrong by Henry Lewis, 1858.

GET ON THE WEB!

The Quad Cities' Web site has links to important historical events and characters as well as to the four cities of Rock Island and Moline in Illinois, and Davenport and Bettendorf in Iowa. Explore **www.qcmemory.org.** Choose "Quad Cities History" on the navigation tool, then start with the timeline to see where the Grand Excursion of 1854 fits in.

legislator, so the town was called Stephenson in honor of a military officer. Local developers soon changed the name to Rock Island.

Anticipation of the railroad connection to Rock Island fueled a frenzy of land buyers and sellers. All hoped to get rich on rising land values. River traffic boomed, bringing 175 steamboats a month to the Rock Island landing during the late spring and summer of 1854. So the five chartered Grand Excursion steamers were not likely to have been the only large boats at the landing.

Construction had already begun on the Rock Island Railroad Bridge, the first structure to span the Mississippi

U.S. arsenal shops at Rock Island, Illinois, 1906.

River. It would take two years to complete. Stretching more than 2,000 feet, it leapfrogged over the island to the fledgling community in Iowa that actually did take George Davenport's name. Railroaders bragged that the bridge was a "mighty triumph of art and enterprise." It cost $400,000 to build, a princely sum in those days.

Steamboat captains had another opinion of the bridge, for it immediately posed the most dangerous manmade obstacle to navigation on the entire Mississippi. They thought the railroad company had purposely built the bridge at an angle to the river's current so that steamboats would be swept against its piers. The danger would make passengers afraid of steamboat travel and want to take the rails instead. Fifteen days after the bridge opened, a large steamer crashed into a pier and caught fire. The steamboat company sued the railroads. The railroad company, on the other hand, held the steamboat company responsible when the fire destroyed the swing portion of the bridge.

Young Abraham Lincoln was one of the railroad lawyers. Arguing that the bridge was legally built, even though it might try the skills of the river captains, Lincoln and the railroad company won the day. In the following year another fifty boats collided with the bridge piers. Five years and many lawsuits later, the U.S. Supreme Court decided once and for all in favor of railroad bridges, whatever their impact might be on navigation. A decade would pass before Rock Island got a new and safer bridge.

Government Bridge of 1872 at Davenport, Iowa, with wagon level above and railroad below, 1906.

BRIDGING THE RIVER

Research a bridge in or near your community to create a timeline of its existence. Include the years when earlier versions of the bridge were demolished and replaced. A good place to start is the book *Crossing the Mississippi Bridge by Bridge*. Then look at a current road map that shows the Upper Mississippi River. How many automobile bridges can you find along the river? Measure the distances between them and calculate the mileage. Make a chart, then graph your findings. What is the longest distance between bridges? What is the shortest? Why are some of these distances longer than others?

STARTING THE JOURNEY

Rock Island was the promising community that welcomed the Grand Excursionists at the town's depot on the late afternoon of Monday, June 5, 1854. An immense throng gathered to cheer them on, then cheered some

Boat	Birth	Death
WAR EAGLE	1854 (Fulton, Ohio)	1870 (La Crosse, Wis., burned)
GALENA	1854 (Madison, Ind.)	1858 (Red Wing, Minn., burned & sank)
GOLDEN ERA	1852 (Wheeling, W. Va.)	1868 (New Orleans, La., dismantled)
G. W. SPARHAWK	1851 (Wheeling, W. Va.)	1856 (St. Louis, Mo., lost in ice)
LADY FRANKLIN	1851 (Wheeling, W. Va.)	1856 (Coon Slough, Wis., snagged)

more as former U.S. president Millard Fillmore gave a brief speech. Band music and cannon fire filled the air as he and his fellow excursionists transferred to the steamboats for the third and final phase of their journey.

Five steamboats set aside for the travelers lay in harbor. The two largest had just been built, and none was more than three years old. All were of the side-wheel type and weighed between 206 and 296 tons. Their lives would be short, which was typical of steamboats of that era. Natural hazards and boiler explosions were often fatal to the boat, if not the passengers.

The *War Eagle,* ca. 1865.

Even this fleet of boats proved unable to handle the ever-growing flock of excursionists, now numbering 1,200. Two more boats joined the flotilla, the *Jenny Lind* and the *Black Hawk.* One was named for the most famous singer of the day, a visitor from Sweden championed by circus showman P. T. Barnum, and the second for the legendary Sac chief.

Nightfall prevented the travelers from stopping at the army island. But to their delight, a grand fireworks display rose from the site of the old fort as they steamed across the river. Four days later, the *St. Paul Daily Pioneer* would report it to be "a scene of surpassing beauty and magnificence."

Their immediate destination was Davenport, on the Iowa riverbank. A great crowd formed on shore. Bonfires lighted the landing and business district, more fireworks went off, and more speeches were made. At ten o'clock, at last tiring from the day's activities, the excursionists filed back onto their boats. A final salvo of fireworks greeted them from the island, and the fleet began its journey up the Mississippi.

The town the excursionists left behind was near the southern end of a long tract of land along the river known as the Black Hawk Purchase. It stretched almost the full length of the modern Iowa border, from the Des Moines River in the south to the Yellow River in the north. The tract had opened to white settlers in 1833.

Antoine Le Claire, ca. 1850.

MAPPING THE BLACK HAWK PURCHASE

Look at a current map to locate the area of land known as the Black Hawk Purchase. Find the three rivers that border the land: Mississippi, Des Moines, and Yellow. Compare the rivers in size, length, and shape. Try to guess where Chief Keokuk's two gifts of land to Antoine Le Claire might be. Hint: One is near the Davenport waterfront; the other is in the smaller city of Le Claire.

The Sac Indians granted the two choicest pieces of land in the tract to Antoine Le Claire, a fur trader who treated them respectfully and honestly. Le Claire was one of the most important and best-liked men on the river. He had mastered a dozen different Indian languages and dialects, and spoke English as well as his native French. His language skills and wide circle of friends brought him the job of official interpreter for many of the Upper Mississippi Indian treaties signed in the 1820s and 1830s. Le Claire used the southern piece of land given to him to establish a ferry to Rock Island. When his friend George Davenport took over the ferry, this tract of land formed the basis of the city that did eventually take the pioneer trader's name. Here are the rates charged for crossing the river:

Man and horse	25 cents
Horse or cow	37 ½ cents
Horse hitched to wagon	25 cents
Carriage, cart, or wagon	one dollar

Even before the Rock Island Bridge was built, Davenport was rapidly surpassing Rock Island as a major supply base for the West. Davenport also boasted more than ten schools and two private colleges, with a women's college on the way. Had the excursionists seen the city in daylight they might have observed dozens of large houses and business blocks under construction. With completion of the railroad connection between Rock Island and the east, the population of Davenport mushroomed to more than 10,000, over twice that of its Illinois neighbor.

After the Civil War, lumber milling became the city's dominant industry. By the time the vast white pine forests had disappeared, Davenport had a large enough industrial base to continue to thrive. The 1910 census showed Davenport to be the second richest city in the nation on a per capita basis.

Not long after the first two settlements were established on either side of the river, a third community arose just upstream from Rock Island. The name of the town was Moline (after the French word for mill, *moulin*), and it used the river not as a means of transportation but as a source of power. In 1841 its pioneer settler, David Sears, built the first dam on the Upper Mississippi, connecting his mill site to the north end of the army island. His dam raised the level of water above the mill, making it fall with greater force over the mill wheel. That was one of the simplest ways to harness the energy of the river. Since the Grand Excursionists steamed up the Davenport side of the island in the dark, they never saw what Sears's endeavors had grown to: four lumber mills, two flour mills, and a city of 1,000 strong.

While Sears was busy trying to capture the power of the river, a Vermont blacksmith named John Deere introduced an industry that would bring Moline an interna-

Ferry boats between Davenport, Iowa, and Rock Island, Illinois, ca. 1925.

FERRYING ACROSS THE RIVER

Create math problems using the rates people paid to cross the Mississippi River by ferry (see page 34). For instance, imagine your family moving from Rock Island, Illinois, to Davenport, Iowa, in 1840. If you think of cars as wagons and family pets as horses, how much would it cost to move everyone and their belongings across the river?

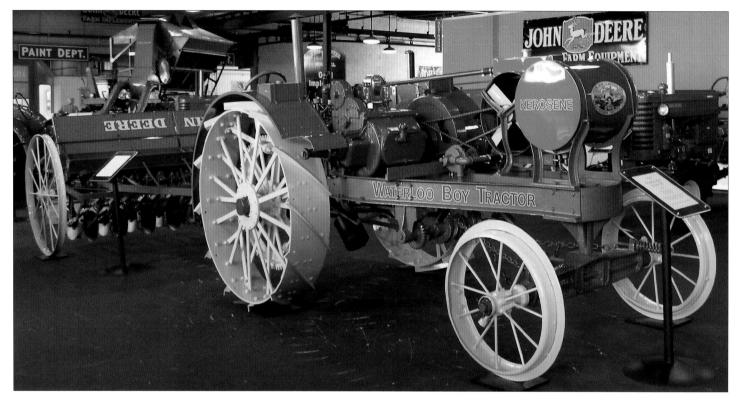

Display of early farm machinery at the John Deere Pavilion in Moline, Illinois.

ALPHABETIZE IT!

Create an alphabet book of the Upper Mississippi River. Next to each letter, write as many words as you can about the river and its people. Use words from this book, but also think of descriptive words of your own. For example, the letter R might stand for Rock Island, railroads, and reporters. The letter M could stand for mosquitoes, malaria, and mud. Illustrate your book with drawings or photographs.

tional reputation. New Englanders had a hard time cutting through the tough prairie sod to plant their crops. It tended to build up on the iron plows they had brought with them to the Midwest. After setting up shop in Grand Detour, Illinois, Deere invented a new type of plow, made of shiny steel so that the soil would fall off as it was cut. Since no new steel was available at first, he used a worn-out saw blade shaped over a log. Deere made only a few plow blades the first year, but by the time the Grand Excursionists passed by he had set up a factory in Moline producing more than 1,000 plows annually. Moline was on its way to becoming the world center for manufacturing farm equipment.

In 1854, Rock Island, Davenport, and Moline were the only large communities in the area. But a fourth town would soon be platted, completing a nest of communities known today as the Quad Cities. Like Moline, this town also achieved a name in manufacturing, but it would have to wait for half a century and several name changes to reach any degree of prominence. At the time Deere was getting his plow business under way, the settlement was called Lillienthal, after the owner of the tavern and dance hall. Shortly after the Grand Excursion took place, the name was changed to Gilbert to honor the man who first platted the town. Finally, just after the dawn of the twentieth century, two brothers named Bettendorf promised to move their iron wagon business from Davenport if the town would give them land along the river for their factory. Townspeople pooled their

money, the factory was built, and the town finally had a distinct identity to go with its new name: Bettendorf.

LE CLAIRE

A few miles north of Davenport is an old river town that once vied with Davenport in importance, if not in size. How Le Claire began was determined almost by accident. An outbreak of cholera raged through Fort Armstrong in 1832, the same year a treaty formally ended the Black Hawk War and soon produced the Black Hawk Purchase. The cholera outbreak required moving the signing ceremony to the mainland, where Sac chief Keokuk would donate the two sections of land to Le Claire. The southern section became Davenport, while the northern section, given to Le Claire's Sac wife, Marguerite, became Le Claire. The

The old Bettendorf Axle Factory in Iowa, viewed from Moline, Illinois.

Looking past the 1851 Old Mill House in Le Claire, Iowa, to Rapid City, Illinois.

The Cody House in Le Claire, Iowa, early in the twentieth century.

only condition of the gift was that the Le Claires build their home on the exact spot of the treaty signing.

The financial panic of 1837 ruined the prospects of the settlement that grew up around the Le Claires' house. What kept the town from disappearing altogether was its strategic location on the river. Rock Island was well known among steamboat pilots for the fifteen-mile stretch of rapids upstream. At the head of the rapids was Le Claire.

Just as the economy nosedived, the U.S. Army Corps of Engineers began to improve navigation in the Rock Island area by removing reefs that turned the main channel into a corkscrew. But straightening the channel did little to quiet the water. It was still so rough that only specially skilled pilots could guide a large steamer through safely.

Several pilots made their living navigating the rapids, and Le Claire was the natural place for them to live. At its prime, it was home to nearly fifty pilots and another fifty steamboat employees such as clerks and stewards. Thirteen pilots' houses have been preserved as the Cody Road Historic District in Le Claire.

The name of the district recalls another historical tidbit about Le Claire. In the 1840s, the parents of famed Wild West entertainer Buffalo Bill Cody moved into the area. By 1854, the Cody family had already moved on to Wyoming, but the town of his birth now memorializes his life in the Buffalo Bill Museum.

One of the museum's best-known exhibits is a section of a rock elm trunk. This was no ordinary tree. It was the Spreading Elm, one of the most famous Upper Mississippi landmarks for more than 100 years. Steamboat employees waited under the shelter of the elm, giving it a nickname: the Green Tree Hotel. Its branches eventually spread 108 feet, and the base of its trunk grew to a circumference of eighteen feet. The mighty tree died from Dutch elm disease in 1964, long after the last steamboat had come ashore.

Above the rapids, the quiet beauty of the Upper Mississippi began to unfold for the Grand Excursionists.

But at the time of their journey, the first northward stretch of the river was already showing signs of the industry and congestion to come.

"Buffalo Bill, Famous Plainsman and Scout," 1952.

The towboat *Jennie Gilchrist* tied up at the Green Tree, Iowa, 1880.

STAYING AT THE GREEN TREE HOTEL

The Green Tree Hotel had the following dimensions: height, 65 feet; spread, 108 feet; circumference of trunk at base, 18½ feet; circumference of trunk at 4½ feet, 13½ feet. Is there a tree in your community that has similar dimensions or is historically significant? The American Forestry Association (**www.americanforests.org**) offers activities for taking a close look at trees. You can even nominate a tree for its list of Historic Trees.

3
STEAMBOATS AND SMOKESTACKS
From Le Claire to Dubuque

Campers on the Mississippi, Dubuque, Iowa.

We were amazed at the crowds that we saw lining the shores, and the glad social shouts of civilized men, at the warehouses and huge hotels, and continuous blocks of build-ings, where but a few years since, was heard only the yell of the savage.

Catharine M. Sedgwick
Grand Excursionist and author

Campers on the Mississippi near Dubuque, by Harger and Bliss, 1907.

Between 1850 and 1870, when the steamboat era was at its height, one of the busiest stretches of the Mississippi River was the run between St. Louis, Missouri, and the Fever (now Galena) River in Illinois. Nearly 100 settlements sprang up along the Mississippi, each dreaming of becoming the next Chicago or the next St. Louis. None quite fulfilled those lofty ambitions, yet many could boast important industries at an early stage in their lives. By the time of the Grand Excursion, shipyards, sawmills, and mining works already dotted the river's shoreline on either side between Rock Island and Galena. Black smoke poured from stacks on both ship and shore. Maps, drawings, paintings, and photographs if anything *exaggerated* the amount of smoke in the air. To many people of that period, billows of smoke were a sign not of pollution, but of progress.

Mississippi River between Albany, Illinois, and Dubuque, Iowa.

to allow the exchange of goods across the river. Without the landings, Iowa would have been able to grow river cities only where bridges crossed the water. Yet only one of these twin towns fulfilled its earlier promise to become a city of major significance on the Mississippi.

Le Claire is the Iowa half of the first set of twins. The river course separating it from Port Byron, Illinois, is so narrow that teams from the two cities hold tugs of war across the water every summer. Port Byron has a wonderful history of names. Its first settlers called it Canaan, the biblical term for "promised land." Then in 1836 a pioneer merchant renamed it after the famous English poet Lord Byron, who had died twelve years earlier. Although it never achieved the fame of either of its names, Port Byron remained an important stop, first for steamboats and then for a railroad line.

MISSISSIPPI TWINS

Between the Quad Cities and Dubuque, Iowa, five consecutive pairs of "twin towns" straddle the Upper Mississippi. All date to the mid-1830s, when land on the Iowa shore first opened for white settlement. The pairing of towns was often created by the need for ferry landings

The other twin towns are Cordova (Illinois) and Princeton (Iowa); Albany (Illinois) and Camanche (Iowa); Fulton (Illinois) and Clinton (Iowa); and Savanna (Illinois) and Sabula (Iowa). Perhaps because of their cross-river connections, all of these twin towns have survived, much of their

Port Byron, Iowa [actually Illinois], and Berlin, Illinois [actually Iowa] by Henry Lewis, 1858.

MAPPING TWIN RIVER TOWNS

On a map of the Upper Mississippi, find all the pairs of towns across the river from each other. Measure the distance across the river between the pairs (for example, between Clinton, Iowa, and Fulton, Illinois). Measure the distance from one pair to another (for example, from Cordova/Princeton to Albany/Camanche). Use the map's scale to compute the distance in miles. Pick a pair of towns without a bridge between. What roads take you from one to the other? How long a trip would it be?

Windmill at Fulton, Illinois, standing on the earth embankment built to protect the town from flooding.

House in Cordova, Illinois, from the early 1850s.

river charm intact. A few, most notably Albany and Cordova, even retain several of the simple buildings that the excursionists of 1854 might have seen above the shore.

Albany was home to Stephen Hanks, one of the most famous pilots on the Upper Mississippi. A first cousin of Abraham Lincoln, Hanks first achieved renown as a pioneer logger and raft pilot on the St. Croix River, which divides part of Minnesota and Wisconsin. By the time of the Grand Excursion, he had joined the Galena and Minnesota Packet Company and was on his way to making a name for himself in steamboating. The Grand Excursion included boats from his company, but so far as is known Hanks was not piloting any on that voyage.

But for a stroke of luck, the city of Clinton might still be an insignificant speck on the map, pretentiously named New York. When the excursionists steamed by, all they could see (if they could see anything at all in the dark) was a scattering of cabins, stores, and taverns. The area's first settler, a New Yorker named Joseph Bartlett, started a ferry service and opened a store in 1835. Believing there was gold in the area, he platted a town the following year, naming it after his home state. When his dreams of gold failed to pan out, he sold his assets and moved away.

Bartlett had given up too soon. In 1855 the success of the Chicago and Rock Island Railroad lured a second railroad into making a river crossing right where Bartlett had set up his ferry. Completion of the bridge brought a fresh wave of New Yorkers, who renamed the town after their state's two-term governor, DeWitt Clinton. The sleepy river settlement sprang to life, expanded its boundaries to absorb other settlements around it, and became the county seat.

By the end of the decade, Clinton was the sawmill capital of the nation. Enormous rafts of logs that were floated downriver from Wisconsin and Minnesota timberlands were cut into lumber at Clinton, then shipped in all directions via the river and the new railroads. Riverboat captains nicknamed the city "Sawdust Town" because of the piles of refuse spilling from the mills onto the riverbanks.

During the lumber boom years, Fulton briefly rivaled its river twin, Clinton, as a port. Like many Upper Mississippi towns, Fulton drew settlers from many nations, but the Dutch made a particularly strong showing. This was appropriate, for flooding often reduced Fulton to an island, and over the centuries no one has learned how to deal with high water better than the people of the Netherlands, a third of whose land is below sea level. As a tribute to this significant part of its heritage, Fulton erected a ninety-foot operating windmill in 1999, designed and assembled in the Netherlands. Craftsmen who had followed it across the Atlantic Ocean put it up on the middle of the Fulton flood control dike.

Log raft arriving at Clinton, Iowa, ca. 1910.

The Lincoln Highway and the new Lyons and Fulton Bridge viewed from Fulton, Illinois, ca. 1920.

CARL FISHER'S DREAM

The bridge at Fulton, Illinois, was part of the first transcontinental road in the United States, promoted by Carl Fisher, founder of the Indianapolis Motor Speedway. Today, U.S. Highway 30 approximates the Lincoln Highway route from Pennsylvania to Wyoming. You can find a complete route map at **www.lincolnhighwayassoc.org.** Locate the eastern and western ends of the highway. How would you travel between those points today? How much time would it take? Find out how fast cars could go in 1913, the year the road was built. How much time would it have taken to drive the complete road back then?

Fulton and Clinton were always closely connected, first by one of the upper river's busiest ferries, then by one of the Mississippi's first railroad bridges. The graceful geometry of the 1891 wagon bridge, designed by local builders, inspired countless photographs and postcards. But it was the automobile that brought about the most famous connection between the towns. In 1912, Carl Fisher, founder of the Indianapolis Motor Speedway, dreamed of a gravel road stretching from New York City to San Francisco. A year later, the Lincoln Highway became the first transcontinental road in the United States, and the new Fulton Bridge carried it across the Mississippi to Iowa and beyond.

The uppermost pair of the river twins are Sabula and Savanna. On the Illinois side, Savanna was settled by a Boston family named Pierce, who lived in an Indian hut while building their house. Pierce supported his family in a way common to many early river men: he cut cordwood for steamboats to use as fuel. From these humble beginnings the town grew to more than 1,000 people by the time of the Grand Excursion. It now has nearly four times that population and boasts a city airport, but it is still very much a river town.

The first white man to set foot on Sabula soil rode a log over to Iowa from the Illinois side of the Mississippi. By the 1840s, several settlers had followed him, although by more conventional means. After experimenting with ordinary names, they decided on Sabula, from the Greek

Lonely Brother Bluff near Savanna, Illinois, ca. 1930.

Sun setting behind Potter's Mill in Bellevue, Iowa.

Causeway to the island city of Sabula, Iowa.

word for the sand they saw everywhere about them. The town used to be part of the Iowa mainland, but in the 1930s the lock and dam system raised the water so high around it that it was turned into an island. Though only four blocks wide and nine blocks long, Sabula has never been flooded.

Halfway between Savanna-Sabula and the Wisconsin border, the town of Bellevue, Iowa, grew up at the beginning of a stretch of river too wide for convenient ferrying. It thrived by serving the rich farmland around it as a flour milling and commercial center. Elbridge Potter built Iowa's first gristmill, which ground wheat into flour, in

1843. Two years later the birth of Jackson County government took place in a monumental Greek Revival courthouse. These structures have survived to anchor Bellevue's heritage of pioneer buildings. The courthouse enjoys a second life as a public school; the mill has been restored and turned into a restaurant and bed-and-breakfast.

As the grain business tapered off, Bellevue took advantage of the lakelike expanse of the river in front of it to become a boating center. Shortly after the beginning of the twentieth century, local machinist Bill Brandt began to produce boats powered by small gasoline engines, including his most famous craft, *Redtop.* When he and his son retired, his stone-walled shop closed its doors for the final time with its machinery still in place. It remains in that condition today.

GALENA AND DUBUQUE

The Grand Excursionists passed Bellevue early on Tuesday morning, June 6. Like many river travelers of their time, they went an hour off course to stop in Galena, Illinois. Though the town is on the Fever (now Galena) River several miles upstream of the Mississippi, it had become a virtual Mississippi River port. The nation's first mineral rush in the late 1820s fueled Galena's growth into the busiest steamboat stop between St. Louis and St. Paul. At the time of the Grand Excursion, Galena's population approached a crest of 14,000, many of the residents deriving their wealth from the lead mines close by the city.

A few years earlier, Maine native Daniel Storer echoed a common sentiment in his diary. "Galena," he wrote, "is the roughest town I ever saw, but a smart business town." The Galena lead mining district, which covered the sides of a series of hills, was barren of trees or brush, cluttered with rubble, and filthy with the dust and mud of mining operations. But that did not keep away the 1854 excursionists, who rode and tramped their way up the hills to marvel at the fortunes being made from gaping holes in the ground. Once more, it was an occasion for grand speeches. Former president Millard Fillmore

Bill Brandt's Iowa Boat and Marine machine shop in Bellevue, Iowa.

Redtop on the Mississippi River approaching Dubuque, Iowa, 1909.

The Lead Region—Galena in the Distance by J. Dallas, 1858.

led the way, followed by Yale natural history professor Benjamin Silliman, former postmaster general Nathan K. Hall, and various politicians, ministers, and journalists. Less plucky excursionists stayed behind to marvel at Galena's grand display of wealth, a collection of houses and commercial blocks that would have been the pride of any New England city. Much of this heritage has been preserved as a National Register Historic District.

Galena is also proud to be the hometown of Civil War general and American president Ulysses S. Grant. Two of his family's homes are open to the public. The one he lived in before the war typifies the simplicity of river town architecture north of St. Louis at the time of the Grand Excursion. The second house was given to Grant and his family by Galena after the war in gratitude for his services to the Union. His wife, Julia, described it as

Ulysses S. Grant residence before the Civil War, Galena, 1866.

Grant residence after the Civil War, Galena, 1866.

ULYSSES S. GRANT'S HOUSES

Look carefully at the pictures on the left of President Ulysses S. Grant's first and second houses in Galena, Illinois. Describe their roofs, their windows, and their entries. Then look up the definitions of Greek Revival and Italianate in the dictionary, an encyclopedia, or an architectural guide to see if your descriptions match the definitions. What are the prominent features of each of these architectural styles?

Look for houses or buildings in your community that have similar styles. Find out the years in which they were built and the names of their architects.

"a lovely villa exquisitely furnished with everything good taste could desire."

Galena gave the Grand Excursion its last sunny weather until it reached St. Paul. As the boats steamed back to the Mississippi from Galena, a heavy rain set in. The travelers naturally expected that few townspeople would greet them at their next stop in Dubuque, Iowa. But virtually the entire population of the city—then 4,700 strong—thronged to the levee. Commercial buildings sprouted with flags, cannons boomed, and the crowds cheered wildly through the usual round of speeches.

Dubuque lies just across the river from the Illinois-Wisconsin border. Like Galena, it began as a lead mining center. French fur trader Julien Dubuque based his

Dubuque, Iowa by Henry Lewis, 1858.

operations there in the 1780s. He lived among the Mesquakie Indians, who introduced him to the lead that abounded in their lands. Out of friendship for him, they granted Dubuque control of a large mining district in 1788. Because Spain claimed the land at the time, Dubuque petitioned the Spanish governor to confirm his possession, naming it the Mines of Spain when the petition was granted. When Dubuque died in 1810, the Mesquakie buried him on a high bluff with honors befitting one of their chiefs. Forty-four years later, the excursionists saw nothing but the bluff itself. Not until 1897 was a permanent marker placed at his gravesite. Designed to look like a castle on Germany's famous Rhine River, the Dubuque Monument has been a prominent Mississippi landmark ever since.

After Dubuque's death the Mesquakie reclaimed the lead mines. But in 1822, well before the land was formally opened to white settlement, the lead rush in Galena spilled across the Mississippi to Iowa and began to exploit the mines. The Mesquakie formally gave up the land in 1833, and 500 more people flocked into the community now bearing Dubuque's name.

The Mesquakie had used the lead largely for ornament. American industry soon put it to many other uses, such as making gunshot. For many years Dubuque mining companies did little with the lead but melt it into seventy-pound blocks called pigs, then raft the lead pigs down to St. Louis, where the gunshot could be manufactured.

Julien Dubuque's tomb, Dubuque, Iowa, 1907.

MINING FOR MINES

Nearly every community has had some kind of mining activity, even if only for sand or gravel. Is mining a part of your town's history? If so, what was mined? Is mining still going on or has the supply of rocks or minerals been depleted?

The old deserted Shot Tower, Dubuque, Iowa, ca. 1930.

But in 1856, two years after the Grand Excursion had passed, the mining companies had a better idea. Why not manufacture gunshot right in Dubuque? Doing that required a tall tower in which the molten lead could form into perfect little balls as it fell. This idea gave birth to another river landmark, the Dubuque Shot Tower. Rising to 150 feet, the tower has the same obelisk shape as the Washington Monument.

Dubuque's steep terrain produced a city with several distinctive landmarks. Businesses and factories occupy a plateau sixteen feet above the Mississippi. But there was little room there for a residential district to grow, so paths and roads were cut into limestone bedrock to carry the city's workers to their homes among the bluffs. For the homes atop the bluffs, stairways as steep as ladders had to be built. One of the most peculiar survivors from Dubuque's early days is a steeply inclined private railroad built to carry a banker from his business to his residence.

Dubuque evolved into the major shipping and railroading center on the Mississippi between St. Louis and St. Paul. A traveler of 1856 thought the city was "more compactly built, and contains a greater proportion of fine buildings than any other place in the state." A good gauge of the city's growth during the time of the Grand Excursion was the explosive rise in ferry traffic. In 1853, 6,200 people used the Dubuque ferry. In the next year that number jumped to 38,400.

Fenelon Place Elevator in Dubuque, Iowa.

LIFE ON THE EDGE

For various reasons, many of the towns on the Upper Mississippi River have reshaped the land they stand on. Find out what has happened over the years to the topography of your town or a town near you. Have hills been removed or low places filled in? What slopes have been cut into for roads?

List as many reasons as you can think of for these changes. Think about these questions: Did any of the changes do harm to the environment or the people in the city? Were the benefits created more important than the harm?

STEAMER "J.S."
ENTERING BRIDGES AT DUBUQUE.

64539

Steamer *J. S.* entering bridges at Dubuque, 1911.

Dubuque's greatest period of growth was yet to come. In 1874 Diamond Jo Reynolds bought a shipyard in Eagle Point, just north of Dubuque. Reynolds already owned a shipping business, a railroad, a flour mill, and a tannery. Before long he became the best known entrepreneur on the Upper Mississippi, and Dubuque established itself as a shipping and boat-building center. Much of Dubuque's

fine present-day collection of old houses and churches dates from Diamond Jo Reynolds's days.

Across the river and tucked into the extreme northwest corner of Illinois lies the little city of East Dubuque. Originally called Dunleith, it enjoyed a brief period of prosperity when the Illinois Central Railroad reached it

POPULATION EXPLOSION

Reread the description of Dubuque, Iowa, on pages 53–56 to recall the reasons that its population exploded in the mid-1850s. Do these same reasons apply to other towns described in the book or does each have its own story for becoming a popular place to live?

Wagon and railroad bridges connecting East Dubuque, Illinois, and Dubuque, Iowa, 1910.

Eagle Point, near Dubuque by Alfred R. Waud, 1872.

READING PICTURES

Historians read pictures to find clues to the past. What is happening in the picture above of Eagle Point? Can you tell what time of day or what season it is? What do you think the artist is trying to express about the scenery, the people, or the activity pictured? What does he reveal about himself in how and what he chooses to depict?

the year after the excursionists had gone by. Three decades later, Mark Twain, humorist and former riverboat pilot, poked fun at the town in his book *Life on the Mississippi,* comparing its residents to "mice nesting in a wheat stack."

After leaving Dubuque, two of the excursion steamboats, the *Galena* and the *Golden Era,* were lashed together to allow passengers to cross between the boats and socialize with their friends. Band music filled the air, and one or more of the main cabins was cleared for dancing. Many of the excursionists were so distracted by the activities that they paid little attention to the river just as the boats entered one of the most stunning passages of its trip to St. Paul. A wilderness already celebrated by painters and writers in the East was just opening to them, yet many passengers would see little of it until the fleet neared the Minnesota border.

Reporter James F. Babcock's letters to his home newspaper in New Haven, Connecticut, show that at least a few of the excursionists continued to look outward in the last light of the day. "Mountains, narrow plains, tangled forests and beautiful groves are sweeping by like a never ending panorama," Babcock wrote. He also recorded the excursionists' first glimpse of Indian life, a group wrapped in blankets who hailed the boat from the shore.

4

THE EAGLE AND THE INDIAN

From the Wisconsin Border to Genoa

Looking upriver from Pike's Peak State Park, Iowa.

Over one hundred and fifty miles of unimaginable fairy-land, genie-land, and world of visions, have we passed during the last twenty-four hours. . . . Throw away your guide books; heed not the statement of travelers; deal not with seekers after and retailers of the picturesque; believe no man, but see for yourself the Mississippi River above Dubuque.

Charles Weldon
Grand Excursionist

*D*ubuque marks the beginning of a strikingly beautiful stretch of the Mississippi River Valley. Although rain chased many of the Grand Excursion passengers into their cabins, those who ventured into the wet evening air of June 6 saw sights they would never forget. Great bluffs arose on either shore, and mysterious islands appeared midstream. Earlier that day they would likely have seen eagles fishing the waters. Eagles have patrolled the Mississippi for as long as humans have camped and hunted on the upland shore. Native cultures celebrated the raptor's presence with dances, songs, clothing, jewelry, and eagle-shaped burial mounds. When the Grand Excursion steamed through, few traces of native human habitation remained. But the area still abounded with Indian lore and the sites of important Indian villages, treaty signings, and conflicts.

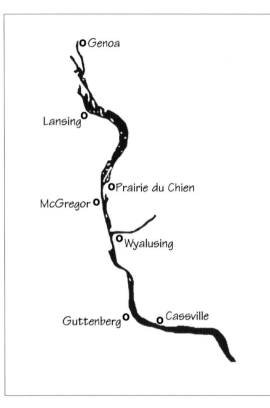

Mississippi River between Cassville and Genoa, Wisconsin.

WISCONSIN MINING TOWNS

What first drew white settlers to this part of the river was neither its ancient lore nor its beauty but the promise of instant wealth. The mining success of Dubuque and Galena lured hundreds of prospectors farther north into Wisconsin, where lead also had been discovered. In fact, the importance of lead mining in early Wisconsin history gave birth to the nickname "Badger State." The miners dug long, narrow burrows in the ground both to mine the lead and to serve as makeshift shelters, in much the same way that badgers dig their homes.

Most of the lead was already extracted by the time the Grand Excursion passed by. The settlements that had staked everything on mining profits vanished as quickly as they had appeared. Most lived so briefly that they are not even called ghost towns, but embryo communities—settlements that had not quite managed to be born.

Sinipee, Wisconsin, was the largest of these settlements. Its history was as tragic as it was brief. In 1831 Payton Vaughn moved with his bride from North Carolina to the eastern bank of the Mississippi River, about three miles north of Dunleith. For a few years Vaughn had great success mining lead. In 1836 he built a grand hotel known to miners and traders up and down the

Buena Vista, a steep bluff between Dubuque and Guttenberg, Iowa, by Alfred R. Ward, 1872.

river. The town that grew up around the Stone House, as it came to be called, appeared ready to compete with Galena and Dubuque. But spring floods submerged the village in 1839, leaving pools of standing water that bred mosquitoes and malaria. All the settlers but the Vaughn family died or moved away. Said one eyewitness in the following year, "When the bankrupted city burst upon our view, a singular sensation took hold of me." Theodore Rudolf (quoted in William Stark's *Ghost Towns of Wisconsin*) continued, "The buildings were all new, showing no sign of decay or deterioration by usage or the weather, having stood there but a little over a year. I expected momentarily to see the occupants come out to bid us welcome." Only the village cemetery and the ruined and overgrown foundation of the Stone House remain.

Eagle Landmark by Elmer P. Peterson, located in Riverview Park, La Crosse, Wisconsin.

Inside a lead mine near Cassville, Wisconsin, ca. 1900.

GHOST TOWNS

Write a story as if you lived in Sinipee, Wisconsin, during the 1830s. Imagine you were staying at the Stone House when the flood of 1839 swept into town. Describe how relieved everyone felt when the floodwaters went away and how that feeling changed when malaria spread through the town. Why do you think the Vaughn family was spared?

Not even that much remains of Lafayette, Wisconsin, once the port for the mining town of Potosi. In its heyday the landing boasted an elaborate wooden wharf and the glorious name "Port of Potosi." From 1836 to 1846 it was the leading port on the Upper Mississippi. Several miles inland, St. John's Mine at Potosi is the oldest lead mine in Wisconsin. First exploited by the Mesquakie Indians in the eighteenth century, the mine is open now as a tourist site during the warm months.

Back in the 1940s, Lafayette Station (the town itself had disappeared) was at the center of a railroad run claimed to be the fastest in the world. Luxurious streamlined trains called Zephyrs ran from East Dubuque, Illinois, to Prairie du Chien, Wisconsin, at speeds of up to 100 miles per hour.

Just upstream, an obscure and brief-lived settlement known as Osceola, Wisconsin, made news in 1945, a century after its last inhabitants had abandoned it. Spring flooding washed Indian relics free of the riverbanks, where commercial fishermen found them. An archaeological dig followed this discovery. More than 5,000 artifacts came to light, some of them more than 3,000 years old. A site that white settlers had given up on in less than ten years had been home to the Woodland Indian culture for more than 2,000 years. Many years after all remnants of Osceola had vanished, its name was taken by a Wisconsin town on the St. Croix River, a tributary of the Mississippi.

Turtle-shaped lead bowl artifact crafted by Oneota Indians.

About thirty miles north of Dubuque, a modern river traveler can finally put in at a town that has survived its pioneer lead-mining beginnings. Cassville seemed destined to become the territorial capital when Wisconsin was formed in 1836. A large brick building financed by eastern investors went up on the main street, intended to house the legislators and state offices. But if the excursionists had stopped by, they wouldn't have found any government officials, for Madison won the capital competition. Cassville's "Big Brick" had just been converted to a hotel known as the Denniston House. It is still the only building in town to reach three stories. Though now empty, it has been preserved as a National Historic Landmark.

The other noteworthy monument in the vicinity was not so fortunate. The man who saved the Big Brick, Nelson Dewey, had become Iowa's first governor in 1848. After leaving office he built a lavish mansion just north of his hometown. But his family did not relish this "palace in the wilderness," so mother and daughter moved back to Madison. The house burned to the ground in 1873, only five years after it had been completed. As a picturesque ruin, it remained a tourist destination for many years, just like medieval castles in Europe. In recent times it has been rebuilt and now serves as a state historic site.

Colonel William Hamilton, the son of statesman Alexander Hamilton, had nominated Cassville to be Wisconsin's capital, claiming that "nature has done all in her power to make it one of the most delightful spots in the far west." A popular 1852 guide to western travel, which some Grand Excursionists likely carried with them, had a more up-to-date view. While Cassville had an especially attractive position on the Mississippi, financial

The Denniston House in Cassville, Wisconsin.

Ruins of Nelson Dewey "castle" near Cassville, Wisconsin, ca. 1920.

ROMANCING THE RUINS

Many ruins already existed along the Upper Mississippi River at the time of the Grand Excursion. Choose one, using the picture on this page and the one of the Shot Tower in Dubuque (page 54) as starting points. Find out more about each original building and why it fell into ruin. Make up a legend about it based on your findings.

woes had turned the town itself into "a dull and dilapidated village," said travel writer Daniel Curtiss in *Western Portraiture and Emigrants' Guide: A Description of Wisconsin, Illinois, and Iowa.*

Eight hundred years before white settlers arrived, the Mississippian people built a great effigy mound in the shape of an eagle on the Cassville site. It is a reminder that some of the best things on the river remain unchanged. The once-proud city may have had to rethink its ambitions, but the town celebrates its excellent vantage points, and eagles still soar overhead. In fact, a few miles upstream the village of Glen Haven has one of the largest eagle habitats on the river.

Another link to the past is the ferry that still crosses to the Iowa side from Cassville. Of the dozens of ferries once connecting small towns in Iowa and Wisconsin, this is the sole survivor. No other means of crossing the river exists for more than fifty miles in either direction between East Dubuque and Prairie du Chien.

WHEAT AND BUTTONS

In Iowa, the first substantial settlement above Dubuque is a quaint little city known as Guttenberg. The French called the site Prairie la Porte, or "doorway to the prairie," because it brings the broad expanses of rolling grassland right to the banks of the Mississippi. It was a common camping ground for Sac and Mesquakie Indians before the Black Hawk Purchase.

Guttenberg owes its beginnings as a white settlement to German immigrants sponsored by the Western Settlement Society of Cincinnati. The townspeople named it after the most famous historical figure from the area of Germany that they had left behind: Johannes Gutenberg, inventor of the printing press. A plat maker's error in 1837 put two T's into the inventor's name, and Iowans have spelled it that way ever since. The city library proudly displays an exact duplicate of Gutenberg's famous Bible, one of 310 printed in 1913.

Partial bird's-eye view of Guttenberg, Iowa, 1869.

By the early 1850s the German settlers had already created a remarkable trove of native limestone buildings, but the grand warehouses soon to follow would become the town's signature. Once used for storing wheat until it could be loaded onto steamboats, each of the three-story limestone buildings has gone through a succession of lives—from pearl button factory or general store to restaurant, hotel, or boutique.

Upstream another twelve miles, the village of Clayton, Iowa, had an even more impressive way of storing grain: more than forty acres of underground caverns reaching deep into the surrounding bluffs. They were originally mined for sand to make mortar, among other purposes. As river traffic tapered off, Clayton's population dwindled from several hundred to a few dozen inhabitants. A devastating fire dealt the downtown its final blow. All that remains today to display its brief period of wealth is a massive old stone school building. The caverns, in the

SEEING LIKE A BIRD

A map or drawing from a bird's-eye view depicts what a place looks like from high above. Choose a place along the river and draw a bird's-eye view of the way it looks today. First make a simple sketch of it. Then refine the details by moving closer to the various parts of the scene. That is how the old bird's-eye views were created.

G. F. Weist's grain warehouse, built around 1854 on the Guttenberg, Iowa, waterfront, later became the Empire Pearl Button factory.

meantime, continue to be used as a major grain storage facility.

Guttenberg and Clayton began to lose importance as shipping centers as soon as the railroads arrived. But then an industry emerged that would reawaken sleepy steamboat towns all along the Mississippi: the manufacture of buttons. The Indians had gathered river clams and mussels for their meat, holding onto the shell to use as a digging tool, much like the modern trowel.

Early white settlers gathered clams and mussels from the riverbed for nothing but the rare chance of finding a pearl. But a machine invented in the 1880s drilled holes into the thick shells and turned the part bored out into buttons that had some of the same mysterious beauty as real pearls.

Suddenly clams and mussels became a prized river "crop." Forty-nine pearl button factories in thirteen cities sprang up from Louisiana to Minnesota, many of them putting long-empty warehouses back into use. Manufacture continued through the first half of the twentieth century until the shellfish beds were depleted and cheaper plastic buttons came onto the market. Few of the old button factory buildings remain. But a sharp-eyed traveler can still find half-buried piles of shells along the shore, each shell punched through with characteristic round holes.

Upstream and across the river from Clayton is Wyalusing ("Home of the Warrior" in the Munsee-Delaware language), a spot renowned for centuries for its sweeping views up and down the river. Only a scattering of buildings remain of the Wisconsin town, once a thriving commercial center of 2,000 people. The arrival of the railroad in the 1880s, a savior for many fading river towns, did Wyalusing more harm than good. The first pair of tracks removed the business district, and the second pair, laid in 1917, took out its remaining riverfront warehouses.

Close by the town is a famous outlook over the delta of the Wisconsin River where it flows into the Mississippi. This is where Father Jacques Marquette and explorer Louis Joliet entered the Mississippi in 1673. They were the first white men to see the upper part of the river. A beautiful state park now lines the bluffs and spills to the shore. It is a wonderful place to see Indian mounds and follow a canoe trail through the backwaters of the Wisconsin River delta.

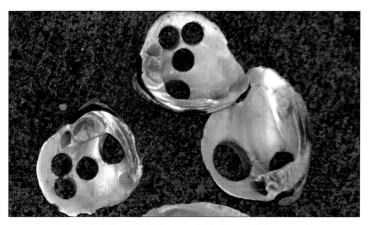

Mussel shells with holes punched for pearl buttons.

WHO'S GOT THE BUTTON?

Take a walk along the Mississippi River bank in one of the river towns. Look for shells with buttons bored out like the ones in the picture above. Research button-making along the Upper Mississippi. Which towns had button factories or clamming operations? How long did this industry continue? What happened to make it go away?

Father Jacques Marquette and explorer Louis Joliet.

Monument to the passenger pigeon at Wyalusing State Park, Wisconsin.

Wyalusing State Park also has an unusual funeral monument, dedicated to the passenger pigeon. Once abundant in Wisconsin and on the river's shores and islands, the passenger pigeon was hunted to extinction. The last one in Wisconsin was shot near Wyalusing in 1899.

Across the river, an area known as Pike's Peak vies with Wyalusing for its dramatic views of the Mississippi. At 450 feet, Pike's Peak is the highest point in Iowa. Near its base arose the colorful town of McGregor's Landing, named for a Scotch-Canadian pioneer who ran a ferry across the river in the 1830s and 1840s. The ferry—and its many descendants—was called the *Rob Roy* after Scotland's national hero. On the original ferry, four mules walking around a circular wheel in the center of the boat drove the ferry forward. At the time of the Grand Excursion, McGregor's Landing was on its way to becoming one of the busiest wheat ports on the Mississippi. Today, known simply as McGregor, it is more commonly noted as the birthplace of four of the Ringling brothers. Their wagon show in 1884 was the start of the Ringling Brothers circus. Though the days of the thriving river port and the Ringling Brothers are long past, McGregor's main street still thrives with shops and businesses, many of them in buildings that date to Grand Excursion times.

A mile upstream, North McGregor amounted to little until the railroads came looking for a place to build a bridge in the 1860s. The town had one thing McGregor lacked: a long piece of low, flat land to receive the end of the bridge. North McGregor (since renamed Marquette) quickly grew into the largest railroad terminus in Iowa, employing about 400 people at the yards.

The Mississippi River is more than a mile wide at Marquette. The islands between the shores possess such scenic beauty that they were once considered for a national park. But the shifting sands of the river around and between them posed problems for bridge building. In 1874, engineer John Lawler devised a way of making two long sections of the bridge float. The section on the Iowa side, nearly 400 feet long, swung open to allow boats and rafts to pass through. This was the first permanent pontoon bridge ever built, and it survived nearly a century, from 1874 to 1961.

FORTS AND WARS

Across the river from Marquette is one of the oldest communities in Wisconsin, Prairie du Chien. French Canadian fur traders settled on St. Feriole Island close to the eastern bank not long after Marquette and Joliet's expedition. When Americans came into the area during the War of 1812, Fort Shelby was established close by on an old Indian mound. This crude fort was the only Wisconsin battle site of the war. After the war the fort was replaced by a massive log blockade known as Fort Crawford, which in turn gave way to a fort built on higher ground between 1829 and 1835. It was one of the most impressive structures on the Mississippi,

Pontoon Bridge and raft at Marquette, Iowa, 1915.

DESIGN A BRIDGE

Look through the book for pictures of Mississippi River bridges. How many different kinds can you find? To help in identifying bridge types, look at the book *Climbing the Mississippi River Bridge by Bridge* by Mary C. A. Costello. Choose your favorite type of bridge design. Draw or sketch it, then make a model with cardboard, toothpicks, or LEGOS.

The B. W. Brisbois Store, now the Fur Trade Museum, in Wisconsin.

THE FUR TRADE

Take a field trip to a fur trade site, such as the museums at Prairie du Chien in Wisconsin and Historic Fort Snelling and the Henry Sibley house in Minnesota. Who were the workers in the fur trade? Was it still a thriving business in the 1850s? What kinds of furs were most in demand? What were they used for?

attracting many artists as well as river tourists and travelers during its brief period of use.

Fort Crawford's most famous moment came when Black Hawk, the leading Sac warrior chief, surrendered there in 1832. His surrender ended the last concerted effort of Indians east of the Mississippi to reoccupy their old lands. The sites where he made his last stand are upstream from the fort and far removed from his people's ancestral lands in Illinois.

Two years after the Grand Excursion passed by, Fort Crawford was abandoned. After a brief reuse during the Civil War, it no longer served a purpose. Like Governor Nelson Dewey's house farther south, it fell into a state of picturesque ruin much visited by travelers until it was finally removed during an extensive archaeological dig in the 1930s. A restored hospital building, detached from the rest of the complex, serves as a museum of the fort's history.

The old part of Prairie du Chien village lay upstream from the fort. Charles Lanman, a traveling journalist of the late 1840s, observed in *A Canoe Voyage up the Mississippi and around Lake Superior in 1846* that its houses were "planted without any order," creating "a rude and romantic appearance which is quite refreshing." One of the rude houses he saw remains today, a log cabin put up by a French voyageur by the name of Vertefeuille ("Greenleaf" in English). Built as early as 1810, it is the oldest house on its original site on the Upper Mississippi.

View of the Great Treaty Held at Prairie du Chien by J. O. Lewis, 1835.

Fort Crawford in Wisconsin by Henry Lewis, 1862.

FORT CRAWFORD AND THE SACS

The painting by J. O. Lewis (top left) shows a large assembly of Sac Indians at the signing of an important treaty in 1825 at Prairie du Chien, Wisconsin. The painting by Henry Lewis (bottom left) shows the Sacs in canoes in the same area in 1848, sixteen years after their final removal from Illinois. Why do you think Henry Lewis continued to show the Sacs living on the Mississippi River? How are they depicted differently in the two paintings? What can you learn about Fort Crawford from the two paintings?

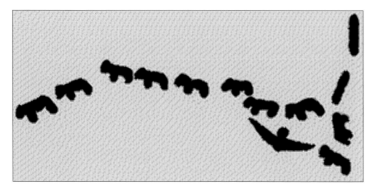

George Catlin sketch of effigy mounds at Effigy Mounds National Monument.

EFFIGY MOUNDS

Look up the word "effigy." What does it mean? Visit **www.nps.gov/efmo**, the primary Web site for Effigy Mounds National Monument in Iowa. Much of the site's information also applies to the mound sites scattered along both sides of the Upper Mississippi River. Many of the mound sites are in state parks. Visit one of them in person. Draw a picture of each mound you observe. What do the shapes remind you of?

That anything at all remains on St. Feriole Island is something of a miracle. At least forty floods have washed over it since the French fur trading post was established. Yet there are significant survivors, among them a stone store building, now restored and used as the Brisbois Store and Fur Trade Museum. Like fur trader B. W. Brisbois's house nearby, the store was there when the Grand Excursion steamed by in the night. Also on the island is the beautiful Villa Louis, an Italianate-style brick mansion built in 1870 by the widow and son of famed fur trader and pioneer Hercules Dousman. The opulent mansion is now owned and operated by the Wisconsin State Historical Society.

North of the bridge connecting Marquette and Prairie du Chien are several parks with magnificent views of the river. The best known of these is Effigy Mounds National Monument in Iowa, famed for its many burial sites in the shape of native mammals, birds, and reptiles. The monument contains 200 mounds altogether, all built by Mississippian Indians between 500 B.C. and A.D. 1300.

Just upstream from the effigy mounds, Paint Rock Bluff was once a conspicuous point of reference for navigating this part of the river. The symbols painted on the rock outcroppings have been gone for many years. At the foot of the bluff is a more modern expression of the river site: Waukon Junction, Iowa, a once-thriving railroad town now noted for its curious collection of houses on stilts to protect against floodwaters.

On the Wisconsin side, Lynxville is a small town that once boomed with river trade. It had bragging rights to assembling the largest object that ever floated down the Mississippi, a log raft covering an area equal to three city blocks. North of Lynxville, the Grand Excursion encountered many of these enormous rafts. The half-dozen men who guided the rafts also ate and slept on them, often for weeks on end. Watching the steamboats pass was one of their few amusements, and they made the most of it, cheering wildly and sometimes firing salutes with their rifles.

Lansing is another of Iowa's picturesque river towns. First surveyed by Nathan Boone, son of famed pioneer Daniel Boone, it was just coming into its own when the excursion passed by. Along the waterfront old and new houses live in quiet company against the background of the Black Hawk Bridge, one of the most beautiful steel span bridges over the Upper Mississippi.

Just before dawn the Grand Excursion passed three small Wisconsin communities marking the final expulsion of Indian peoples to the west side of the river. The first of these, Winneshiek's Landing, began as a trading post shortly after the treaty of 1832. Among the Winnebagos (Ho-Chunks), Chief Winneshiek had legendary status as a leader they thought destined to preserve their rights and lands. His own people knew him as Wau-kon-chaw-koo-haw, meaning "the coming thunder." But the Winnebagos had been gone for many years by the time the town was laid out in 1854, and it was sited directly over an old

A typical stilt house on the river in Waukon Junction, Iowa.

STILT HOUSES

Why are some houses near the river built on stilts? What would it be like to live in one? Imagine getting to and from your house by boat during high water. Make a house from cardboard using craft sticks for the stilts. Don't forget to create a way to get up to the house from the boat!

De Soto, Wisconsin, by Henry Bosse, 1891.

Winnebago burial ground. The founders of the community were so set on having a pure New England colony that all "foreigners" were kept from buying property or establishing businesses. Curiously, the founders named their town De Soto for Hernando De Soto, a Spaniard who had "discovered" the Mississippi River for the Europeans in 1541. Their plans for ethnic purity went awry when a lumber mill attracted the usual mix of immigrants, and the little town at the base of the bluff joined the melting pot that the American nation had become.

By the 1850s the Black Hawk War was already part of regional folklore. Two new Wisconsin communities,

Black Hawk Bridge and the city of Lansing, Iowa.

The Battle of Bad Axe by Henry Lewis, 1858.

MAPPING BLACK HAWK'S WAR

On road maps of Wisconsin and Illinois, find all the sites associated with Black Hawk and the conflict of 1832: Rock Island (site of Black Hawk's birth and early life), Prairie du Chien (treaty site), and Victory, Bad Axe River, and Bad Axe, now Genoa (battle site). If you travel to Genoa and Victory, look for the six historical markers that tell about the final conflict.

Victory and Bad Axe, each carried names that reflected their area's role in Black Hawk's last struggle. After a chase from Illinois into Wisconsin, Black Hawk's surviving band was stopped by a gunboat as it tried to return to the west side of the river. Ninety percent of the people with him, many of them women and children, died in this final conflict.

The village of Victory never outgrew its small beginnings, but Bad Axe City, named after a river where much of the fighting took place, prospered. The maps available to the Grand Excursionists continued to identify the settlement known simply as Battle Field. But as immigrants from northern Italy flowed into the area after the Civil War, they put their own stamp on the community by rechristening it Genoa, the birthplace of Christopher Columbus. This "bit of the Mediterranean beside the Mississippi" (a popular description of unknown origin) became a fishing town reminiscent of the peaceful hillside villages of the Italian immigrants' old country.

Bird's-eye view of Genoa, Wisconsin, ca. 1905.

5

From Minnesota's Border to Lake Pepin

Homer, Minnesota by John T. Sperry, 1869.

That portion of the Mississippi which extends from Prairie du Chien to Lake Pepin is the most mountainous and truly beautiful on the whole river. . . . The river here varies from a quarter to a full mile in width, and on either side throughout the whole distance is a range of mountains which sometimes actually bend over the river, and sometimes recede into the interior for several miles.

Charles Lanman
A Canoe Voyage up the Mississippi and around Lake Superior in 1846

Near the Iowa-Minnesota border, the Upper Mississippi River Valley undergoes a dramatic change. Tall bluffs continue to offer spectacular views of the waterway, but they also assume spectacular forms themselves. Rather than run in continuous ridges, they draw away from each other at intervals and sometimes draw back from the river itself. Their wondrous shapes have fired the imagination of Indian native and white settler alike, who attached names to them like "Mountain Dipping in Water," "Sugar Loaf," and "Chimney Rock." In the nineteenth century, many traveling writers and artists even saw in the rock formations resemblances to ancient ruined castles along the Rhine River in Germany.

Even though the Grand Excursionists viewed much of the Upper Mississippi landscape through the rain or darkness, the dramatic shape of the bluffs made a deep impression. Reported writer and passenger Catharine Sedgwick in the "The Great Excursion to the Falls of St. Anthony": "The surpassing beautiful marvels of all are the mimic castles, or rather foundations of ruined castles, that surround the pinnacles. These mere rocks of lime and sandstone so mock you with their resemblance to the feudal fortresses of the Old World, that you unconsciously wonder what has become of the Titan race that built them!"

As the bluffs draw away from the Mississippi and back again, they form long, narrow valleys known as coulees. Settlements that sprang up at the riverfront of the coulees had commanding views, not only of the water but of the vast, grassy prairies to the west. Several of these communities evolved into important agricultural centers as well as river cities.

Mississippi River between Brownsville and Wabasha, Minnesota.

New Albin, Iowa, shows how much the shape of the river can affect a young settlement's history. The town came to life in 1868 as Jefferson, Minnesota. But the bluff that towered behind it allowed no room for it to grow, so in 1872 the townspeople moved many of their buildings and businesses across the border to make a new town. On the north edge of the new settlement they found an old cast iron monument marking the Iowa-Minnesota border. Hauled by horse and sled across the frozen river in

1849, the monument showed them that they had arrived in Iowa. The marker is still in place, half-hidden behind a new building.

Just upstream, the Mississippi bends and twists through a course of water known as Coon Slough. At one time Coon Slough posed the greatest natural hazard to navigation on the entire river. Years of dredging finally straightened the channel, and the dam below it raised the water to the doorstep of a nearby farming community, Stoddard, Wisconsin, converting it into a river town.

Brownsville is the first Minnesota community the Grand Excursionists were likely to have seen. Spread along the curving base of a towering bluff, Brownsville had just been platted into streets and lots. A U.S. Land Office attracted early settlers to the town to inquire about farmland. At the turn of the twentieth century, Brownsville had a unique role on the Upper Mississippi as the operation headquarters of the University of Minnesota Center for River Studies.

LA CROSSE

Once it had left Dubuque, the Grand Excursion planned only one more "general" stop—that is, a stop in which everyone was expected to go ashore. La Crosse, Wisconsin, was the scheduled port, and on Wednesday morning, June 7, the flotilla kept to its plan despite a driving rainstorm. A large crowd assembled on shore, and when former president Millard Fillmore appeared on the

The 1849 Iowa-Minnesota boundary marker near New Albin, Iowa.

MOVING A TOWN

Find New Albin, Iowa, on a current map. Make a guess as to the original location of the town. How do you suppose the buildings were moved? Have buildings in your community been moved? Check out the International Association of Structural Movers Web site (**www.iasm.org**) to learn about the history of house moving.

Lacrosse Players by Elmer P. Peterson, La Crosse, Wisconsin.

deck of the *Golden Era,* he was greeted with prolonged cheers. He made only a brief speech before the fleet hurried on.

Though La Crosse still had the rough look of a lumber town, it was rapidly becoming the commercial center of western Wisconsin and southern Minnesota. Nathan Myrick built the first cabin on an island in the river in 1841. A year later he moved to the mainland and laid out his village. The name he chose, La Crosse, was the French term for a ball game played by Indian peoples through much of Canada and the northern United States.

The city's future was ensured when the La Crosse and Milwaukee Railroad reached the Mississippi River not long after the Chicago and Rock Island Railroad. Today La Crosse has a metropolitan area with nearly 100,000 people, a branch of the University of Wisconsin, and the varied population and economy of any sizable urban center.

Sometimes the dreams of new settlers caused them to do strange things. Across the river from La Crosse, fur trader Peter Cameron set up the trading post of Manton in 1851. Convinced that his crude log buildings would grow into a metropolis, he and a small crew set about digging a canal that would drain a large swampy area for settlement. By the time the Grand Excursionists steamed by, his scheme was already running into difficulties. But he and the townspeople did not give up entirely on their dreams of rivalry with La Crosse. Thinking that

La Crosse got its name from the Christian symbol on banners and flags during the Crusades in the Middle Ages, they chose a symbol used by Muslim armies in the Crusades, renaming their town La Crescent.

Some of Cameron's excavation for the canal is visible today, but the city has gone in a much different direction than his grand plans. La Crescent now takes pride in being the "Apple Capital of Minnesota."

In the years just preceding the Grand Excursion, a long row of Minnesota communities squeezed into the narrow, linear space against the bluffs below Winona. Richmond, at the base of Queen's Bluff, has long since disappeared. But many writers were taken by the unusual character of its site. As R. E. Garczynski wrote in *Picturesque America* in 1872, "Queen's Bluff has not only been cleft in twain by the greater Mississippi of the past, but its face has been reopened out by the winds, and Nature has kindly filled up the gloomy void with trees."

A little farther upstream, George Dresbach founded a more successful community at the base of Mineral Bluff. He quarried limestone from the nearby hills for use as building material. The stone itself became known as Dresbach limestone, and the village also carried his name. While many of the river communities around it disappeared, Dresbach not only survived but continued to prosper.

Castle Rock near Winona by Elmer and Tenney, ca. 1870.

COMPARING BLUFFS

Look through this book for pictures of river bluffs, such as the one above. Compare how the artists and photographers have depicted them. How are they the same? How are they different? Notice the colors, lighting, and composition, as well as the scene itself. Choose the picture you like the best. Why is it your favorite?

Landing and warehouses at La Crosse, Wisconsin, ca. 1910.

ACTION ON THE WATERFRONT

Look at the picture above of the busy river landing at La Crosse. Discover all the activities that are going on. Look for multiple kinds of transportation, the various work being done, and the different ways people are dressed. Why do you think the tracks at the front of the picture are covered with boards? Can you see telephone poles? What businesses might be in the buildings on the left?

Across the river from Dresbach, fur traders had established a post in the 1820s. Thirty years later enough of a settlement had grown up around it for it to be platted into lots. The town developer called it Monteville (French for "Mountain City"), which is how the Grand Excursionists knew it when their flotilla stopped by to refuel. The rain had stopped, and many passengers took advantage of the break in the weather. While wood was being loaded onto the boats, the postmaster invited his village visitors to climb Eagle Cliff, a steep bluff behind the village, to see the prairie extending beyond.

Many excursionists accepted the challenge, and half a dozen succeeded in clambering to the peak. But according to William Tibbals, a pilot on the *Galena*, President Fillmore's daughter, Abby, did them one better. She mounted a horse and galloped to the top. When she appeared at the summit, the steamboats all blew their whistles and the crowds onboard cheered wildly.

All who completed the climb were rewarded with a view of what reporter James F. Babcock of New Haven, Connecticut, described as a "prairie of green, stretching away for miles, with the surface broken only here and there by the plow." Many years later Tibbals remembered Abby Fillmore's observation that the river itself seemed to be all islands and that she

Trempealeau Mountain viewed from Perot State Park, Wisconsin.

Trempealeau, Wisconsin, viewed from the south, ca. 1905.

RIDING THE BLUFFS

Imagine Abby Fillmore riding a horse to the top of the bluff behind Trempealeau village (above). Do you think journalists reported this incident because she was President Fillmore's daughter or because it was unusual for a young woman to be such a daredevil in those days? Abby died of cholera just a month after going on the Grand Excursion. Find out more about her in *Children in the White House* by Christine Sadler and on the White House Web site (**www.whitehouse.gov**).

"did not see how in the world the pilots found their way through the myriad of channels, all seemingly alike."

One island Abby saw was among the most famous spots on the Upper Mississippi. It was the only island to rise to the height of the bluffs on either side of the river. The Dakota called it "Moved Mountain," while the Winnebagos dubbed it "Soaking Mountain." Even the French fur traders, who arrived as early as 1685, had a colorful name for it: *la montagne qui trempe a l'eau,* or "the mountain dipped in water." The British shortened this last name to Trempealeau.

A lavish picture book of 1872 called *Picturesque America* prominently featured the mountain and the village. "This little place," wrote R. E. Garzynski, "ought to be visited by every painter and poet in America. . . . It is grief that Americans should wander off to the Rhine and the Danube when, in the Mississippi, they have countless Rhines and Danubes." Monteville by then had been renamed Trempealeau after the mountain. Its mill soon failed like others on the Mississippi because of the irregular flow of the water, and an 1888 fire destroyed its business district. Yet the townspeople rallied to save six of the buildings and move them together to form the heart of a new downtown. One hundred years later their efforts were rewarded by the placement of the Main Street District on the National Register of Historic Places.

Not long before Trempealeau was platted, one of its most prominent settlers, Willard B. Bunnell, moved across the river to Minnesota with his wife, Matilda. They named their new community after Homer, a famous poet of ancient Greece. Their hometown in New York had that name as well—along with towns in fourteen other states. The Bunnells' quaint Gothic Revival cottage survives today as a house museum operated by the Winona County Historical Society.

Willard Bunnell house and museum in Homer, Minnesota.

Queen's Bluff by Henry Bosse, 1885.

The Soaking Mountain on the Upper Mississippi by Jacob C. Ward, 1836.

THE SMALLNESS OF HUMANS

Many nineteenth-century artists liked to portray nature as an overwhelming presence, with people merely bystanders or onlookers. Henry Bosse's photograph of Queen's Bluff (top left) and the print of Trempealeau by Jacob C. Ward (top right) are two good examples. Why is a lone man shown in Bosse's photograph? Who are the people shown in Ward's print? What do you think they are they doing? Make up a story about what you see in each picture and share it with your classmates. How is your story different from the others? Which story do you like best? Why?

The sudden growth of white settlement along the Upper Mississippi occasionally tempted crooked businessmen into creating "paper towns." These were pretty sketches and descriptions of towns drawn up to lure investors but never intended to become real settlements. The rise and fall of Minneowah between 1853 and 1855 is one example. Its name was based on a common mispronunciation of a Dakota expression for "falling water." A fancy map showed a town spread over 318 lots along the river. But people who visited the land they *thought* they had bought discovered that it occupied a slope rising almost straight up the side of a 500-foot bluff. Wrote Wheeler Sargeant, Wabasha County's pioneer historian, "Except the unimportant items of locality, buildings and inhabitants, it had all the characteristics of a great city."

A similar ruse fooled New York and Chicago investors several miles north. Newton, Minnesota, took its name from a local steamboat wreckage. Its promoters developed an elaborate plat, showing magnificent boulevards and sites for churches, hotels, businesses, and residences, as well as ample preserves for parks. Those who were naive enough to purchase land sight unseen later found only a scattering of crude cabins—and the wrecked steamboat still thrusting its name in vivid colors above the waterline to mock their venture.

Just about the time the sun set that Wednesday evening, the excursionists would have had their first glance of a Minnesota settlement that was in fact on its way to

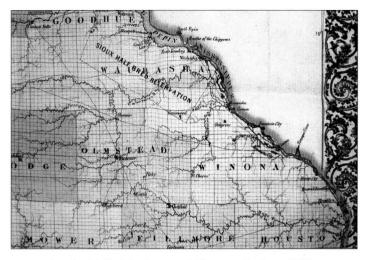

Detail of J. H. Colton's map of Minnesota Territory, 1856.

PAPER TOWNS

Create a river town on paper. Using a current map, locate an area on the Upper Mississippi that has no town. Would this be a good place for a new town? Why? Give it a name and draw a plan for it. Create an advertisement. What will you say about your town to get people interested in moving there? How much will you charge for building lots?

Winona (artist unknown), ca. 1870.

greater things. French fur traders knew the area as La Prairie aux Ailes, or "Prairie of the Wings," and early river men called it Wapasha's Prairie after the powerful Dakota chief. The excursionists' guidebooks (if they had had them) would have used the village's modern name, Winona.

White settlement of Winona began in 1851, when steamboat captain Orrin Smith dropped off three of his men to develop a site for steamboats to wood up. It quickly grew into an important lumber town. At first, townspeople chose the Aztec name Montezuma, but soon they switched to an Indian name with more local roots. *We-no-nah,* the Dakota word for "eldest daughter," was the subject of a famous legend. According to the story, a young girl of that name leaped to her death from the river bluffs when she was forbidden to marry the Indian brave she loved. The bluff where this was said to have taken place was on the other side of Lake Pepin, but the legend was so widespread and so familiar to Dakotas and white settlers alike that any new settlement on the lake could have carried her name.

Winona soon established itself as the largest urban center in southeastern Minnesota. When the state was still a territory, important institutions were divided among its main cities. St. Paul got the capitol, Minneapolis the university, and Stillwater the prison. By the time Minnesota achieved statehood in 1858, Winona was large enough to earn the state's first "normal school," the term for places where teachers were trained.

Not all pioneers liked where they first settled. In the dead of the winter of 1852, an advance party of New Yorkers representing the Western Farm and Village Association skated up the river from La Crosse to form a new village just north of Winona. Calling it Rolling Stone, the land agents drew up the appropriate fancy maps, sold plats, and offered promises of a "good country and rich soil." As many as 3,000 New Yorkers rushed westward to join them in the spring.

Unfortunately, the winter venturers had mistaken a slough for the main channel of the river and a marsh for rich bottomlands. The settlers had to wade through miles of wetlands before settling on a narrow reach of solid ground six miles from the nearest landing. One of

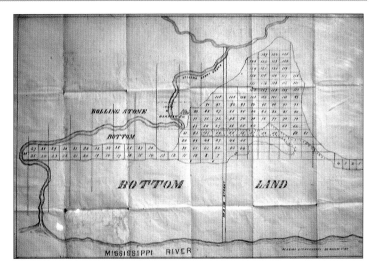

Plat map of Rolling Stone, Minnesota, showing "bottom land" that was actually under water.

them found their destination "a barren, sandy, desolate-looking place, recently burnt over. Would not give ten cents an acre for the whole of it." Most either returned to their old homes or found suitable farmland away from the river. Those who stubbornly remained in Rolling Stone renamed it Minnesota City.

Even the settlers who loved their new land often had itchy feet. Among the best known of the wanderers was Thomas Holmes, who established communities on the Mississippi and Minnesota Rivers before leading settlement parties farther west. His Wisconsin settlement, known at first as Holmes' Landing, grew into Fountain City. It was soon renowned for its grand river views, as well as abundant hillside springs that gave it its name. Rather than squeezing into the base of Eagle Bluff, the

Fountain City, Wisconsin, in 1908, now a repair base for locks and dams.

VISIT A LOCK AND DAM

The Upper Mississippi has fifteen lock and dam systems, which create a "stairway" of water between St. Paul and the Quad Cities. Find out why there are so many locks and where the first one was built on the upper river. Visit a lock and dam near you. Call ahead to find out when a barge or boat will be "locking through." For more information, surf **www.greatriver.com** and its links.

city stretched up the sides. The incline is so steep in places that even upper residents have a clear view of the river, much like those sitting in an amphitheater. For many years Fountain City has been the main service base for the St. Paul District of the U.S. Army Corps of Engineers. Here the corps renovates and paints barges and also makes and repairs much of the equipment for the lock and dam system.

Across the Mississippi in Minnesota once again, the village of Minneiska ("white water") sprang up on one of the finest natural boat landings on the river. But the bluffs cramped its growth. Like many towns in this area, it extends some distance along the river but is only a block wide. Communities like this are known as "string towns." A disastrous fire destroyed most of the village during a brutal cold snap in 1884. After rebuilding, Minneiska remained a small community but in recent years has succeeded in attracting a diversity of small businesses. As in other towns up and down the river, these businesses are now linked to suppliers and customers by the highway rather than by river or rails.

The most dramatic example of a string town along the Upper Mississippi is on the Wisconsin side just below Lake Pepin. Alma stretches its two-block width seven miles along the river. Born in the 1840s as a wooding-up spot, it was known for many years as Ten Mile Bluff. Lumbering operations on the nearby Chippewa River brought the town prosperity and continuous growth throughout the nineteenth century. A few miles north lay Beef Slough, a branch of the Chippewa that became the most famous log-sorting and raft-building area on the Upper Mississippi. Repeated damming of the Chippewa River has shrunk Beef Slough to a shallow backwater, but the heritage of buildings its operations helped to create in Alma remains strong.

In recent years, the Alma area has become a favorite place to watch the spectacle of tundra swan migration. Arriving in mid-October, they fill the Mississippi and its backwaters for a month and more with their glistening white form and soft whistling sound. Once they finish feasting on aquatic plants, they spread their seven-foot wingspan and fly to their winter quarters in the South.

Relief carving depicting tundra swans in flight, Winona, Minnesota.

RETREATING BLUFFS

As the Grand Excursionists approached Lake Pepin it was well after nightfall, but they might have glimpsed lights from a cluster of makeshift houses on the Minnesota shore. Wabasha, the oldest white settlement in Minnesota, stands on a flat expanse of land at the foot of the lake. Many years earlier, a fur trader named Augustine Rocque established two trading posts in the area. As he was the nephew of famed Dakota chief Waupasha (actually, there was a succession of chiefs bearing that name), a name for the larger of Rocque's two posts was easy to come by.

Though well established in the early 1840s, Wabasha was

BIRD WATCHING

The Upper Mississippi Valley is a famous migration route for birds. Discover what kinds of birds use it. Make a chart showing their names, length, wingspan, diet, breeding grounds (where they are in the summer), and wintering grounds. Use the Audubon Society and U.S. Fish and Wildlife Web sites to find information about migrations and bird-watching events.

not divided into lots until 1854, the year the Grand Excursion flotilla steamed by. The town's first downtown building was a log cabin constructed in Mendota, Minnesota, then floated downstream on a raft. Initially used as a chapel, then as a schoolhouse, the cabin stood at the head of Main Street. This started a trend of constantly changing building uses in Wabasha that has continued to the present day. Some of the downtown businesses proudly display information about the many owners and uses of their buildings over time.

When the railroad ran through Wabasha in 1871, the city's future was ensured. Several brick houses of the railroad era, along with the heart of the old downtown, have been honored with a National Register listing. The lowlands north of Alma and around Wabasha mark another great change in the complexion of the Upper Mississippi to a northbound traveler. As the bluffs push farther and farther away from the river, the Mississippi swells toward them. This great widening of the river above Wabasha is known as Lake Pepin.

Delta of the Whitewater River filling the base of a coulee just above Kellogg, Minnesota.

6

LAKE PEPIN AND BEYOND

From Read's Landing to Red Wing

View of the Upper Mississippi by Ferdinand Richart, 1865.

The white man has not yet made his mark upon Lake Pepin and its surroundings; and there lay its calm water, and yonder uprose its mighty watch-towers in all their primal beauty and grandeur.

Adolph Hoeffler
Artist-journalist, 1853

Entering Lake Pepin is one of the most riveting experiences of any trip up the Mississippi. All of the picturesque bays and backwaters suddenly merge with the central stream into a vast, uninterrupted expanse of water twenty-two miles long and as many as three miles wide.

In 1680 Father Louis Hennepin claimed to be the first white man to set eyes on the lake. He invented a fanciful name for it: "Lake of Tears." According to one story, the name was inspired by his observation of a young Indian woman on shore mourning the loss of her husband. In fact, its name has a far less romantic origin. In 1679, two French fur trappers, the Pepin brothers, came upon the lake. They claimed descent from the famed French monarch Pepin the Short, father of Charlemagne, so they honored him (and themselves) by giving the lake their name.

At the foot of the lake, Augustine Rocque established an even earlier fur-trading post than his larger one at Wabasha. But it failed to attract settlers, so he sold it to

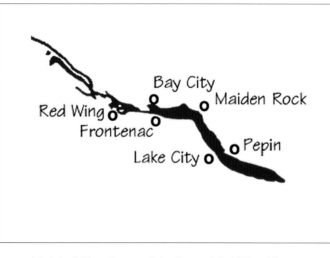

Mississippi River between Lake City and Red Wing, Minnesota.

Charles Read in the late 1840s. Though trained as a soldier, Read knew a valuable piece of real estate when he saw it. The Chippewa River empties into Lake Pepin through a broad delta on the Wisconsin side. Since the delta is low and vulnerable to flooding, the spot was not suitable for a town. So when logs were floated down the Chippewa to the Mississippi, the loggers looked to the Minnesota side for supplies, lodging, and entertainment.

Read's Landing was just on the verge of becoming a boomtown at the time of the Grand Excursion. At its peak just after the Civil War, the community boasted twenty-seven hotels and twenty-one saloons.

In 1870 the town built its one lasting architectural monument, a large brick school that today houses the Wabasha County Historical Society. But Read's Landing soon suffered the fate of all towns dependent on a single industry. That year, completion of a railroad through lumber land to Eau Claire, Wisconsin, pushed Read's Landing out of the picture as a supplier of goods and materials. In 1871, the railroad line along the Minnesota shore bypassed the town altogether. By 1882, Wabasha had earned the right to the railroad bridge that crossed to Wisconsin. Read's Landing

Lake Pepin from Chimney Rock by E. E. Edwards, 1859.

completed its transition from boisterous lumber town to a quiet spot on the river awash with more memories than business.

The Grand Excursionists passed Read's Landing and entered Lake Pepin an hour before midnight on Wednesday, June 7. This time they lashed together four boats of the fleet, all abreast, and danced into the wee hours. This was the perfect place to do it, as no rapids, islands, or shifting channels demanded the crew's attention. According to reporter James F. Babcock, several

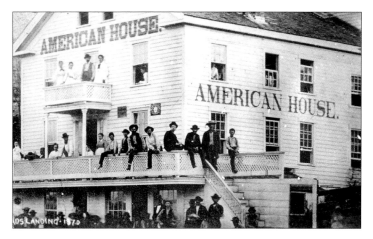

The American House at Read's Landing, Minnesota, 1870.

Lake Pepin from Wabasha by Clement Haupers, 1949.

PARTYING ON PEPIN

Imagine four steamboats lashed together. Draw a picture of what the connected boats might have looked like. Besides dancing, how do you think the excursionists entertained themselves? Several excursion boats run on the Upper Mississippi. What entertainments do they offer? Which are built to look like old steamboats? Do any run by steam power? Use the Web sites listed on page 124 to find more information.

ladies promenaded past the tables where the journalists were gathered, urging them to "spare no adjectives" in describing the wonders of the afternoon and evening.

Running upstream the length of Lake Pepin took about two-and-a-half hours by steamboat at full throttle. Even allowing for a slower speed during the excursion festivities, the lake was well behind the revelers by dawn. Perhaps they thought its landings had little to offer. Maps of the period show half a dozen steamboat stops, most of them barely more than that. A few months later, Maine native Daniel Storer would pass through and remark in his diary, "There are no towns of much account on Lake Pepin." All but Red Wing at the northern end were either trading posts or wooding-up spots with barely a hint of the villages and cities they would become.

Some people who traveled on the Upper Mississippi before the Grand Excursionists even found the great peacefulness of the lake troublesome. A writer for the *Ladies' Repository* in 1846 claimed that "it does us good to look upon a picture like this. At the same time we confess that we should not abide here too long; its peace would unfit us for the conflicts and purposes of real life."

If it had been daylight the travelers would also have glimpsed Indian life along the river, as the Dakota still occupied much of the land. A tract known as the Sioux Half Breed Reservation ran along the Minnesota side of Lake Pepin. Set apart in the Treaty of Prairie du Chien, it guaranteed people of mixed Indian and white blood a place to live. Then the Treaty of Traverse de Sioux, signed just three years before the Grand Excursion took place, pushed Minnesota's Dakotas onto two reservations well west of the Mississippi. But an amendment in 1853 extended the time by which the Dakotas had to leave the lands of their ancestors. So several camps, hunting parties, and half-occupied villages still dotted the river-bank at the time of the Grand Excursion.

Maps available to the excursionists showed only a single settlement on the Wisconsin side of Lake Pepin. Though not yet platted, the village of North Pepin was already something of a steamboat boomtown, a gateway to the vast pineries on the Chippewa River. For a while North Pepin looked like it would control the transfer of lumber from the Chippewa to the Mississippi. But the low river of 1857–1858 made it impossible for steamboats to approach the landing. Then new, light-draft steamboats made it unnecessary to transfer goods at North Pepin for delivery up the Chippewa. The major lumber companies built their warehouses across the lake at Read's Landing, and North Pepin's fate as a lumber town was sealed. But the town's allure as a lakeside community was too well established for it to wither away. With its name shortened to Pepin, the town attracted flocks of summer visitors keen on using its splendid harbor, shops, and hotels while boating and fishing on the lake.

Though the steamboat traffic is now long past, Pepin

maintains its place at the heart of the life of the lake that shares its name. Building up a road through the Chippewa delta created a series of deep troughs. Initially scars on the landscape, these have become favorite sites for deer and waterfowl during the warm months. Pepin residents have also been actively concerned about the health of the river. In the 1970s, Pepin resident Dorothy

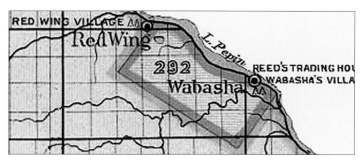

Detail of J. H. Colton's map of Minnesota Territory, 1856.

MAPPING LAKE PEPIN

Draw a map of Lake Pepin. Using this book's text, mark the main steamboat stops along the lake in 1854. On a modern road map, mark the cities and villages with landings on Lake Pepin. Look for campgrounds and other places that also have boat landings.

Pepin, Wisconsin by Isabel Hillman.

RIVER TOURISM

Design a poster or travel brochure featuring your town. What events and sites would you advertise? Illustrate it and include a slogan that captures something distinctive about your town that would attract visitors.

Hill headed up the Citizens for a Clean Mississippi, an organization that mushroomed beyond her town's locale and helped bring about a dramatic recovery of the lake's water quality.

For young readers across the country, Pepin has another claim to fame. At its outskirts stood the log cabin where Laura Ingalls Wilder, author of the *Little House on the Prairie* books, was born. The reconstructed cabin attracts thousands of tourists each year.

Back on the Minnesota shore of Lake Pepin, Lake City grew up during the boom in immigration to Minnesota just after the Grand Excursion. But unlike many towns born during these flush years, Lake City managed to stay alive by constantly reinventing itself. It began as a grain port, then lost much of its downtown to a fire in 1882. Its splendid harbor created two additional opportunities: river clamming for the local population and summer vacationing for Twin Cities residents. At first, the clams were sorted through for their pearls, and many of these brought high prices out East. But when the pearl button industry came to town, Lake City's clamming operation shifted to the shells themselves.

After World War I, with many of the clam and mussel beds nearing exhaustion, Lake City reinvented itself a third time. Sporting enthusiast Ralph Samuelson bought two pine boards, gave them an upward curve at one end, and attached them by a rope to his brother's boat.

By the end of that summer of 1922, Ralph was being towed by an airplane and was on his way to national fame as the inventor of water skiing. The site of an annual celebration of Samuelson's feat, Lake City has become a favorite port for pleasure boating on Lake Pepin.

The same spring that the Grand Excursionists steamed up Lake Pepin, a small group of Swedes landed on the eastern shore. They called their new home Stockholm, after the capital city of the land they had left behind. Their leaders were two brothers, Eric and Jacob Peterson. Eric had come to America several years earlier to join the California gold rush. But he changed his mind when he got to the Wisconsin pineries. After a few years as a lumberjack, he found the perfect spot of land to settle. Returning to Sweden, he gathered 200 of his friends

Crowd at Lake City, Minnesota, watching Ralph Samuelson water ski, 1925.

Lake City Ice Yacht Club by H. G. Rinkel, 1898.

RIVER RECREATION

Visit a spot along the Mississippi and observe the water sports you see people enjoying. Brainstorm a list of all the water sports people participate in today. Would the Grand Excursionists have enjoyed these? Learn more about the history of water skiing at **www.waterskihalloffame.com.**

Trunk belonging to Eric Peterson, the first settler of Stockholm.

and relatives. Half died of cholera before they reached Chicago; the remainder formed the basis of Stockholm. It is the oldest Swedish settlement in Wisconsin.

Several settlers got so discouraged that they moved their houses across the ice to Lake City. Those who held on until the railroad arrived in the 1870s had an unexpected bonanza. The lake ice became the basis for a new wintertime industry. Workers streamed into town to harvest it for shipment to large cities on the Burlington Railroad line.

PACKING A TRUNK

Imagine your family is moving to a new place and can take only one trunk. How will you choose what belongings to take? What would you need for working and living? Would you pack a keepsake to help you remember your friends and former home? Make a list of important belongings. Visit a history museum to look at immigrant trunks and the items people packed.

Many years later an equally unexpected event put Stockholm into the spotlight. In July 1938, Swedish royalty came to America to celebrate the 300th anniversary of Swedish settlement. Crown Prince Gustav Adolf, Prince Bertil, and Princess Louise were on their way to the Twin Cities from Delaware, where Swedish settlement began in America, when they heard of the tiny old settlement in Wisconsin. Their surprise visit was the highlight of the town's history.

Sixty-five years later, Stockholm has a population of fewer than 100 people, but summers make it seem much larger. The sidewalks stream with tourists patronizing its flourishing shops and arts and crafts events, including the annual Stockholm Art Fair.

RESORT COMMUNITIES

Near the upper end of Lake Pepin is an enchanting

Minnesota community that grew up near the site of the old French Fort Beauharnois. The first American settlement in the area was a simple trading post dating to 1839. In the following decade, Israel and Lewis Garrard, sons of the founding family of Cincinnati, Ohio, bought a large tract of land along the shore with little more in mind than having a beautiful place to hunt and fish during the summer months. Dutch immigrant Evert Westerveldt soon established a post office nearby, giving it and the fledgling community his own name.

Westerveldt and the Garrard brothers each built residences just after the Grand Excursion passed by. Known as St. Hubert's Lodge (after the patron saint of hunters), Israel Garrard's home became the social center of an informal summer community that grew up around it. Westerveldt Post Office became Frontenac, and Garrard settled into his new home as a year-round resident. After the Civil War, Frontenac became so popular as a resort area that it was nicknamed "the Newport of the North," after the famous summer settlement in

St. Hubert's Lodge, Israel Garrard's summer house, in Frontenac, Minnesota.

Rhode Island. Visitors included such national figures as President Ulysses S. Grant, publishing giant William Randolph Hearst, famed preacher Henry Ward Beecher, and popular stage actress Marie Dressler.

When the railroad came through, the village's residents did not want it to disturb their summer solitude, so the tracks were routed several miles to the east. A new community sprang up around the railroad depot, taking on the name Frontenac Station. Today, the two Frontenacs, old and new, remain separated by acres of state park wilderness. Neither developed far beyond their simple beginnings. Even "New Frontenac" boasts

a church and several houses dating from its post–Civil War beginnings. With the exception of two bed-and-breakfast businesses, Old Frontenac remains serenely free of commercial activity. It is the first Minnesota community to be placed in its entirety on the National Register of Historic Places.

Not to be outdone by its Minnesota neighbor, a town across Lake Pepin attempted to establish its name as a Wisconsin resort community. Its founders called it Saratoga, the name of the famed resort area in upstate New York. Perhaps because they lacked the pedigree of the Garrard brothers, they never succeeded in attracting

On the beach at Frontenac, Minnesota, ca. 1880.

View along the Mississippi River near Maiden Rock by Edwin Whitefield, 1856–1859.

THE LEGEND OF MAIDEN ROCK

Legends often have more than one version. Find as many retellings of the legend of Winona's leap as you can. Who are the characters? Why is she not permitted to marry the man she loves? What options does she have? Where does the story take place before she leaps from the rock? Which is your favorite version of the story? Why? Write a modern version of the legend.

Frontenac's breed of clientele. After years of being known simply as Bay City, the less pretentious name was formally adopted in 1866. The community today has much of the open, massive cottonwood growth that must have characterized its earliest years.

While easterners were trooping to the Upper Mississippi versions of Newport and Saratoga, a young eastern visionary by the name of John D. Trumble tried to capitalize on the region's most famous Dakota legend. A new Wisconsin settlement was struggling to survive a few miles above the place where Winona was said to have

House perched above the retaining wall that keeps the bluff in place at Maiden Rock, Wisconsin.

leaped to her death. Trumble bought up the town and named it Maiden Rock, after the site of Winona's leap. It grew into a small fishing village, then virtually froze in time. As with many of the towns along Lake Pepin's bluffs, it is difficult to imagine Maiden Rock finding space to grow much larger. The road through town threads its way along a narrow ledge of rock, with most of the houses built just above or just below the ledge.

The most successful community on Lake Pepin ended up being at its head, where one of the villages of Dakota chief Red Wing was located. Daniel Storer, a Maine native, found Red Wing in 1854 "a fine romantic looking place." The steep, rocky hill that towered above it was known as Barn Bluff, after the French name La Grange. By the time of the Grand Excursion, some of Chief Red Wing's people remained, but their quiet village had been transformed into a bustling river town. In the decades that followed, the city would become the river's largest wheat port.

Barn Bluff was already a favorite theme of artists, as it soon would be of photographers. Among Minnesota scenes, only the Falls of St. Anthony and Minnehaha Falls could compete with it. For Red Wing it served as Mount Fuji did for Tokyo, Japan, as a looming presence in the background for an endless variety of town views.

Commercially secure, Red Wing established itself as a cultural center as well. Hamline University, Minnesota's oldest college, opened its doors a few months after the

Barn Bluff, Red Wing, Minnesota by Edwin Whitefield, 1856–1859.

Red Wing by Paul Kramer, 1984.

Red Wing riverfront at the base of Barn Bluff, 1860s.

BARN BLUFF THEN AND NOW

Look at the three pictures of Barn Bluff and Red Wing. What do they tell you about how the town changed as it grew? What businesses do you see? Keeping in mind that each artist accentuates some details and leaves others out, how do you think Barn Bluff itself has changed?

THE VANISHING INDIAN

When Minnesota became a territory, Mary Eastman and her husband, soldier-artist Seth Eastman, lived at Fort Snelling and knew the Dakota (Sioux) Indians well. In her 1849 poem, Mary Eastman expressed her fears that the Indians would disappear: "Give way, give way, young warrior—/Our title would you seek?/'Tis 'the rich against the poor/And the strong against the weak.'" Why did she think the American Indian would disappear? What was happening at the time? Her prediction did not come true. Find out about American Indian communities or reservations in your state. What Indian peoples are represented?

Lake Pepin, Upper Mississippi by Jacob C. Ward, 1846.

Grand Excursion steamed by. (Sixteen years later Hamline relocated to St. Paul.) A women's college, Red Wing Seminary, soon followed. Magnificent houses and churches lined the residential streets. Had the excursionists come ashore in daylight, they would have seen the first settlement on the Upper Mississippi that looked and felt like a bustling New England town in the making. Long after steamboats ceased to dock at its landing, the town expanded its agrarian base to include numerous industries. Among the most famous were a pottery and a shoe manufacturer that still carry the Red Wing name.

With dawn only a few hours away, the Grand Excursion approached the final stretch of river separating it from its destination of St. Paul. It was an area of vivid contrasts. Many remnants of Indian civilization remained, often mixed with white communities already booming with commerce and the beginnings of industry.

7
THE EDGE OF CIVILIZATION
From Hastings to St. Paul and Minneapolis

St. Anthony and the four-year-old town of Minneapolis across the river are situated at the end of civilization. North of these two places the only inhabitants are Indians, bears, and wolves.

Marie Hansen-Taylor, 1859

St. Anthony Falls by Ferdinand Richart, 1857.

*J*ust before day broke on Thursday, June 8, the boats on the Grand Excursion wooded up one last time. Their stop, Prescott, was a fast-growing Wisconsin settlement at the opening of the St. Croix River into the Mississippi. Prescott's meteoric rise would mirror the history of myriad Mississippi River towns in the 1850s.

The first record of a white person visiting the Prescott site was in 1805, when the U.S. government sent Zebulon Pike to drive British traders out of the Upper Mississippi area. Pike camped at the site on his way up the river. Twelve years later Stephen Long considered the site for a military post, but he ultimately recommended a place upstream with a more commanding view. The new military post was Fort Snelling, located where the Minnesota River flows into the Mississippi. Meanwhile, St. Paul merchant Philander Prescott was offered the St. Croix River site to establish a trading post for the fort's officers.

For a decade, Prescott's business struggled. But then the boom times of the 1850s arrived. Stillwater began to send a steady stream of logs down the St. Croix, and

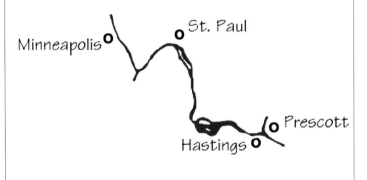

Mississippi River between Hastings and Minneapolis, Minnesota.

steamboats delivered droves of new settlers and their families. The year of the Grand Excursion found Prescott's three hotels, its warehouses, and its private residences all packed with newcomers waiting for their own homes to be built.

As long as steamboats dominated the river trade, Prescott flourished as a shipping and boat-building center. When the twentieth century arrived and railroads threatened river commerce with extinction, it looked like Prescott might lapse into obscurity like so many other river towns. But the birth of steel barges, and the lock and dam system that accommodated their travels up and down the river, gave the town new life. Retired steamboat captains were brought back to train new pilots, and Prescott once again became a river workers' town.

Excursionists who were up and about early that Thursday morning might have made out a number of Indian camps and villages still hanging on to their old sites on either shore of the Mississippi. As steamboat captain George Merrick described Prescott in 1854, "Two hundred white people were planted among 500

Chippewa [Ojibwe] Indians, with as many more Sioux [Dakota] of the Red Wing band across the river in Minnesota." These Indian families refused to abandon their ancestral lands after many treaties had promised them support for resettling in reservations.

In 1889, the federal government finally acknowledged their presence with the creation of a new reservation in Minnesota called Prairie Island. As the reservation's Web site notes, Prairie Island's main claim to fame today "is one no one would really like to have." A nuclear power plant was built in the 1970s just a few hundred yards from the small reservation. This instantly turned the reservation into a legal battleground for

The Mouth of the St. Croix River by Henry Lewis, 1855.

A modern view of Henry Lewis's painting, Prescott, Wisconsin.

SAME AND DIFFERENT

The two pictures above show the same location on the Mississippi River, but they were created 150 years apart. Compare them, looking closely at details. On a piece of paper, draw two intersecting circles, big enough to write in. Label one circle "1850s" and the other "2004." List details that are different in the appropriate circle. List similarities in the part that overlaps.

We-no-na (first born) by the Whitney Gallery, ca. 1865.

Indian woman near Trempealeau, Wisconsin, by Hoard and Tenney, 1875.

INDIANS THROUGH TOURIST EYES

These photographs of Upper Mississippi River people were taken to sell to tourists and others curious about American Indians. How do you see them depicted? Think of reasons they might have been willing to pose. What is the woman doing in the photo on the top right? Use the objects around her as clues.

struggles between environmentalists and suppliers of electrical energy.

Also across the river from Prescott were the bare beginnings of another white settlement. In 1850, Alexis Bailly started a trading post there. Two years later, Bailly and his son, together with their friends Alexander Ramsey and Henry Sibley (both of whom would become governors of Minnesota), met in a hotel to decide on the village's name. Sibley put his middle name, Hastings, into a hat. When his slip was drawn, Hastings became the name of the settlement.

At the time of the Grand Excursion, William G. Le Duc was running a thriving bookstore business in St. Paul. It was a remarkable effort in a settlement that barely had schools. Le Duc did something equally remarkable in Hastings: he built a Gothic Revival mansion that became one of the most famous buildings in the state. It was based on the design of a well-known house on the Hudson River in New York. Travelers from the East Coast often compared the picturesque banks of the two river valleys, so perhaps that is why Le Duc chose the design.

By the end of the Civil War, Hastings was rapidly becoming one of the Midwest's major wheat market places. The grand domed courthouse of this era still stands, along with many of the Main Street buildings that embrace it. But the most unusual public structure in town, a wooden bridge across the Mississippi that spiraled down to

William Le Duc house in Hastings, Minnesota.

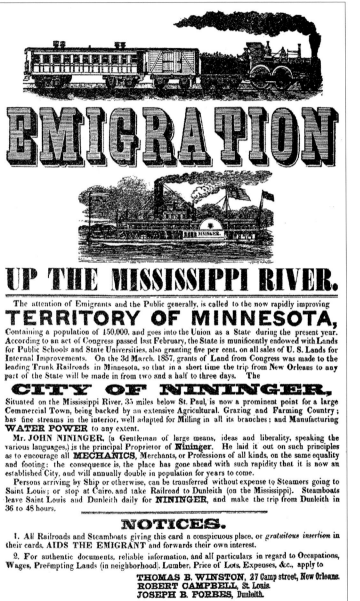

Poster promoting the city of Nininger, Minnesota.

Main Street, was demolished in 1955. Built for wagons in 1894, then adapted for automobiles, it was the subject of popular photographs and postcards.

Minnesota's most famous failed community, Nininger, arose three miles up the river from Hastings. Though it had yet to be established when the excursionists steamed by, Philadelphia native Ignatius Donnelly dreamed of a great midwestern metropolis and tirelessly promoted the new town across the country. By the end of 1857 Nininger boasted numerous stores and churches, a dance hall, a school, a population of 1,000—and the only baseball club in the territory. But that year a nationwide financial panic set in, and Nininger's settlers pulled up their claim stakes as rapidly as they had set them out. By the time Minnesota achieved statehood in June 1858, Nininger was on its way to becoming a ghost town. Several of the grandest houses were moved to the landing, then rafted downstream to Hastings. But Donnelly, who later became prominent in Minnesota politics, stubbornly remained in his house overlooking the town. Now that also is gone.

Thirty years after the Nininger boom had come and gone, a reef called Nininger's Bar grew into the navigation channel just below the town site. On close inspection, Nininger's Bar proved to be made mostly of sawdust and bark that had accumulated from sawmills upstream on the Mississippi River. To restore the channel, the U.S. Army Corps of Engineers packed rocks and branches into a sequence of long, thin piles reaching from the shore like fingers. These wing dams, as they were called, forced the river to narrow its course, making the water run faster. The faster flow of water scoured the sawdust out of the main channel, ensuring that it would remain open and deep.

In 1854 the riverbanks between Hastings and St. Paul continued to show remains of Indian camps, but an alert northbound steamboat passenger could have sensed the approach of a sizable community, for numerous landings also dotted the shore. Grey Cloud, Pine Bend, Red Rock, and Kaposia all grew up on the site of Dakota villages. Grey Cloud would eventually be absorbed into the city of Cottage Grove, and South St. Paul would eventually pull the two northernmost of these settlements within its boundaries.

The Grand Excursionists were filled with anticipation as they approached the final bend in the river below St. Paul. Reporter James F. Babcock of New Haven captured the experience of the hundreds of travelers seeing the city for the first time. "There it is, lying well up on a plat of land about thirty feet above the river, with streets leading down the bank to the shore," he wrote. "There we see five or six churches and a building much larger than the State House of New Haven. It is of brick, a main building and two large wings. That imposing structure is the Legislative Hall of the Territorial Government of Minnesota. Here are ample streets, upon which are all kinds of

Pine Bend, wing dams below St. Paul, Minnesota, by Henry Bosse, 1891.

DAKOTA VILLAGE NAMES

Several Dakota villages south of St. Paul are listed on this page. Try to find out how they got their names or make up a story about how each was named.

buildings of moderate pretensions. The city bears all the marks of youth, for it is but six years old."

To the excursionists, Babcock's description would have seemed overly flattering. St. Paul's public buildings and churches were impressive enough. But the muddy, unpaved streets rutted with wagon tracks, the hodge-podge of houses laid out in a pattern that twisted along the river, and the building debris everywhere showed how close St. Paul still was to its pioneer beginnings.

On one historical point Babcock was slightly mistaken. The village was six years old, but as a city St. Paul had just incorporated that spring. Yet the new city was plainly booming, even without the impetus of the Grand Excursion. As historian Henry Castle noted, "The season

CAPITOL, ST. PAUL.

Crowd at the Territorial Capitol, 1857.

of 1854 was one of unprecedented prosperity for the young city, as well as for the entire territory. Navigation opened on April 6, and a heavy immigration poured in."

ARRIVING IN ST. PAUL

At eight o'clock on Thursday morning, June 8, the flotilla steamed up to St. Paul's lower landing, whistles blowing and bands blaring. The *Golden Era* led the way, with the others following at regular intervals. A local journalist reported a "scene of excitement which St. Paul has never before witnessed." Even the sun seemed to sense the importance of the occasion, for it came poking through the clouds after three days of steady rain.

The city had been planning its reception of the excursion for two weeks. On May 29, the *Daily Minnesotan* declared, "It becomes St. Paul to appear in its best dress on the morning of June 9." The local press urged business owners to lay plank sidewalks and to make carriages and wagons available to visiting excursionists. Five leading citizens of the town formed an arrangement committee. Five more civic leaders were appointed to attend the travelers from their boats to the capitol building, and five more to help the visitors to their proper places at the capitol. Local citizens could attend a gala event in the evening for the exorbitant price of five dollars, which would admit one gentleman and two ladies. This was not an occasion for ditch diggers or stable hands or, in fact, any of those who had labored to build the city of St. Paul.

St. Paul by J. M. Stanley, 1853.

For all of its planning, however, the people of St. Paul were taken by surprise. Warnings from earlier steamboats that the fleet might arrive on June 8 had gone largely unheeded. Railroad companies were well known for bragging about how quickly they could transport people over long distances, yet no one could have anticipated how hurriedly the excursion boats would rush to their destination. Visits to Dubuque and La Crosse had been cut short by rain.

To make matters worse, the excursion party put ashore with little intention of staying around town.

Years later, local journalist T. M. Newson recalled how chaotic things were. "Such a scene! They rushed up Third Street, pitched headlong into the old American House, the starting point of the stage, climbed up on the coaches, hired every hack and every carriage and cart they could find, at enormous figures, in order to reach St. Anthony and see the Falls before the boat made a return trip. The citizens were paralyzed. They put every vehicle they could find at the command of the visitors, but the crowd was so great and the rush so ill-timed, and so inconsiderate, and so unexpected, that it was a mixed and

The Grand Excursion Arriving in St. Paul by David Geister, 2002.

PLANNING THE CELEBRATION

Plan a party for guests who have never been to your community. What would you want them to see? Brainstorm a list of ideas, then figure out how you'd go about making arrangements. What committees would you need? Compare them to the committees that welcomed the Grand Excursionists in 1854. Interview someone who has planned a festival in your community to discover all the details involved.

hodge-podge affair. . . . They were received as hospitably as the circumstances of the case would permit, but many of them went away mad."

Some excursionists wandered about town or put up their feet in the American House or the Central House. Others investigated local sites, such as the cave that English explorer Jonathon Carver had camped in eighty-eight years earlier. Carver identified the cave as a sacred place among local Indians, who called it Wakon-Teebe, or the "dwelling place of the Great Spirit." For years it was the city's most celebrated relic of antiquity. It did not fare well as a tourist destination, however. A rock fall had nearly sealed its entrance, and when the St. Paul and Chicago Railroad ran its line by the cave's mouth, much of the cave disappeared with the hill into which it was carved.

TO ST. ANTHONY FALLS

After their arrival in St. Paul, the majority of excursionists—several hundred in number—took the cross-country ride to the Falls of St. Anthony, near the birthplace of Minneapolis. In the words of author and passenger Catharine Sedgwick, "You should have seen how we—some among us accustomed to cushioned coaches at home—could drive merrily over the prairie in lumberwagons, seated on rough boards. You should have seen the troups and groups scattered over St. Anthony's rocks." One member of the party, a Colonel Johnson, ceremoniously poured water collected from the Atlantic

Ocean a week earlier into the churning waters below the falls. The falls themselves, with their drop of only twenty feet, must have disappointed those looking for a western Niagara.

Excursionists who wrote of their adventure made little mention of the village next to the falls. The settlement that would become Minneapolis, on the west side of the river, had but one house, and in 1854 its streets and blocks were just being laid out. But on the east side, the village of St. Anthony already had a sawmill and its first commercial flour mill. In another twenty-five years, St. Anthony, by then absorbed into Minneapolis, would become the flour-milling capital of the world. On their return to St. Paul, the party traveled on the Minneapolis side, first to see Lake Calhoun and then to

Pioneer and Democrat newspaper office, St. Paul, 1858.

hike down to a beautiful little waterfall called Minnehaha, or "laughing water," by the Dakota. Later that month New England poet Henry Wadsworth Longfellow began writing an epic poem, *Song of Hiawatha,* which ultimately brought visitors to the falls by the thousands. Scores of prints and photographs of Minnehaha Falls turned it into an icon of the Northwest (as the region was known before it was called the Upper Midwest), capturing in a single image the area's primitive beauty and the passing of Indian people and their way of life.

Dakota Indians at Minnehaha Falls by Benjamin Upton, 1857.

Undoubtedly, many excursionists from the East Coast looked down their noses at the conditions under which St. Paul's early citizens lived. But many pioneers were equally amused at the ways of the city slickers. Years later, stories still circulated about a young visitor from Boston who wondered who furnished the whitewash for the birch trees and about another who was puzzled at how all the cows got chewing gum.

At five o'clock, the excursionists reassembled in St. Paul for a trip upstream to Fort Snelling. What most impressed them was not the fort itself but its magnificent setting. A year earlier, sketch artist–writer Adolf Hoeffler (the 1850s equivalent of today's photojournalists) had marveled in *Harper's Monthly,* "The rock upon which it stands is almost as white as marble, and appears in fine contrast with the rich green foliage and the dark walls of the fort. . . . From one of the bastions of the fort, a magnificent view is obtained of the high rocky banks of the Mississippi, with St. Paul in the distance; the broad and fertile valley of the Minnesota; the meeting of the waters; the fort and its appurtenances within and without; Sioux villages, and the wide and gently rising prairie stretching away westward to undefined boundaries." Catharine Sedgwick was also struck by the kindness with which the fort's officers treated the excursionists. "Courtesy and gallantry," she wrote, "are the twin virtues of military life."

As the sun set, the churches of St. Paul rang their bells to welcome the excursionists to the evening's festivities. At

St. Anthony Falls by Herrmann J. Meyer, ca. 1853.

St. Anthony Falls, Great Northern Bridge, and Milling District, ca. 1910.

FALLS VS. FALLS

Some Grand Excursionists were disappointed when they reached the Falls of St. Anthony near Minneapolis. The falls did not come close to the splendor or size of Niagara Falls in New York. The best that could be said about St. Anthony Falls was that they were "wild." Find a picture of Niagara Falls, still a popular tourist site today, and make your own comparison to what the excursionists saw.

St. Anthony Falls is very different today than it was in 1854. Research the falls to find out what changes have occurred and why they happened. If you live in or visit the Twin Cities, take a tour of the falls.

Fort Snelling by Henry Lewis, 1850.

Interior of Fort Snelling by Adolf Hoeffler, 1853.

LIVING THE EXCURSION

Historic Fort Snelling is a living-history museum managed by the Minnesota Historical Society. Visitors step back in time and talk with costumed guides portraying officers, soldiers, fur traders, and other people from the fort's early days.

Create your own living-history museum about the Grand Excursion with your friends or classmates. Find out what kind of clothing was popular in the 1850s and try to create costumes from old clothing or clothing from a costume shop. Make up scenes that might have happened on the trip. Read newspaper accounts of the excursion at county and state historical societies to help you plan.

last the citizenry was allowed to put on a full show. The *Daily Democrat* burbled, "Before nine o'clock an assemblage was gathered within the walls of the Capitol such as was never before seen in this or any other place. The eminent of the land, the fairest flowers of beauty. Age with its bowed form, youth in its strength." Dinner commenced in the hall of the Chamber of Representatives, and the Council Chamber echoed with speeches of such notable excursionists as former president Millard Fillmore, historian George Bancroft, congressional delegate Henry Sibley, and territorial governor Willis Gorman. The evening climaxed upstairs with a grand ball in the Supreme Court Room.

However glorious the festivities, nothing was more important to railroad companies than being on time. Promptly at eleven o'clock, with the dancing barely under way, the organizers of the excursion gave a signal, and the passengers left the party to reassemble at the landing. By midnight, all were back on the river, bound for the return cruise to Rock Island or St. Louis and home.

A CAPITAL MOMENT

The Grand Excursion brought St. Paul its first moment in the national eye. Glowing reports back east, focusing more on its promise than its presence, would fuel the settlement boom of the next few years. Yet it would be two decades before the thriving commercial center anticipated in both St. Paul and St. Anthony would be delivered, and the means of delivery would not be the river but the railroads. In the 1880s, the Twin Cities of Minneapolis and St. Paul, by then connected by numerous rail lines, evolved into the major supply base for westward expansion across the Great Plains and the Rocky Mountains to the Pacific Coast. Railroad and wagon bridges also spanned the river to the north and east, allowing St. Paul to grow beyond the hemmed-in area around its steamboat landings.

In recent years, the Mississippi River has reclaimed its defining presence in both cities. Industrial wasteland along the shores has been converted to boulevards and parkland, and more public buildings and functions are finding homes along the river. In St. Paul, the Science Museum of Minnesota looks over the expanse of river between the old steamboat landings. In Minneapolis, the Mill City Museum oversees the heart of the old flour milling district near St. Anthony Falls. As in so many cities along the Upper Mississippi, the mighty river is once again a vital partner in shaping the urban environment.

Passing under the Wabasha Street Bridge in St. Paul.

More River Activities

RIVER BOATING

Visit **www.steamboats.org** to learn the parts of a steamboat on an interactive model. Then draw your own steamboat, including all of the parts shown on the model.

RIVER BOXING

Use a shoebox to create an Upper Mississippi River diorama. Decorate the outside as if it were a theater. Paint a background inside to show the scenery and wildlife the Grand Excursionists might have seen. You can also show the different kinds of human settlement and activity that took place on the shore. Make a cutout of a steamboat from heavy paper or cardboard to show the 1854 excursion. When you are finished, stand the box on its side in the lid and tell the story of the diorama to a friend.

RIVER PERSONIFICATION

Read about some of the natural occurrences and human events in the Mississippi River's history. Imagine you are the river. Write a biography of a part of your life as a river, or create a story based on a particular event. Remember to write in first person. Tell the story to your family, a friend, or your class.

RIVER POETICS 1

Make an acrostic. Start with a river word running vertically on the page. Write in words or phrases, each one beginning with a letter of the river word. Think of words and phrases that can be connected to make a poem. Here is an example:

E—Elegantly; A—America's symbol; G—glides;
L—loftily: E—Eagle

RIVER POETICS 2

Cut a piece of paper into the shape of the river. Draw islands and dams on it. Write a poem or a descriptive narrative about the river. Fit the written lines between the banks of the river and shape them around the islands. The dams could mark breaks between stanzas or paragraphs.

RIVER THEATRIX 1

Read the following passage from chapter 2 of Mark Twain's *The Adventures of Tom Sawyer:*

"Ben [Rogers] was eating an apple, and giving a long, melodious whoop, at intervals, followed by a deep-toned ding-dong-dong, ding-dong-dong, for he was personating a steamboat. As he drew near, he slackened speed, took the middle of the street, leaned far over to starboard and rounded to ponderously and with laborious pomp and circumstance—for he was personating the Big Missouri, and considered himself to be drawing nine feet of water. He was boat and captain and engine-bells combined, so he had to imagine himself standing on his own hurricane-deck giving the orders and executing them:

"'Stop her, sir! Ting-a-ling-ling!' The headway ran almost out, and he drew up slowly toward the sidewalk.

"'Ship up to back! Ting-a-ling-ling!' His arms straightened and stiffened down his sides.

"'Set her back on the stabboard! Ting-a-ling-ling! Chow! ch-chow-wow! Chow!' His right hand, mean-time, describing stately circles—for it was representing a forty-foot wheel.

"'Let her go back on the labboard! Ting-a-ling- ling! Chow-ch-chow-chow!' The left hand began to describe circles.

"'Stop the stabboard! Ting-a-ling-ling! Stop the labboard! Come ahead on the stabboard! Stop her! Let your outside turn over slow! Ting-a-ling-ling! Chow-ow-ow! Get out that head-line! LIVELY now! Come—out with your spring-line—what're you about there! Take a turn round that stump with the bight of it! Stand by that stage,

now—let her go! Done with the engines, sir! Ting-a-ling-ling! SH'T! SH'T! SH'T!' (trying the gauge-cocks).

"Tom went on whitewashing—paid no attention to the steamboat."

Note the actions, sounds, and commands Ben Rogers uses to imitate a steamboat. Using your body and voice, create the sounds and actions of a working steamboat. Be creative! Watch a video of a steamboat in action (see "River Resources," page 126). How did you do?

RIVER THEATRIX 2
Use blue painter's masking tape to create the shape of the Mississippi River on the floor, or use chalk to draw it on the sidewalk. Dance, run, hop, or skip up and down the length of the river. Now mark where the cities and dams are. Make up a game called "Mississippi River Hop-Scotch" based on these marks.

RIVER THEATRIX 3
Try to make the shape of the river with your body. Several people can do this together to make a long human river.

RIVER RAPPING
Put a rhythm to a list of Upper Mississippi town names and chant them like a rap. Make up a melody or use a familiar tune like "Yankee Doodle" to sing the towns in order from south to north, alphabetically or in any order you choose. Memorize it and perform it for someone.

River Resources

WEB SITES

AMERICAN FORESTS (www.americanforest.org). Lesson plans about trees and conservation.

AMERICAN RIVERS (www.americanrivers.org). Interactive. Click "River ABC" for games, experiments, and a river glossary.

AUDUBON SOCIETY (www.audubon.org). Under "Issues and Actions," click "River" for information about the Upper Mississippi River Campaign, the Audubon Ark, and the Great River Birding Trail.

BIG MUDDY ADVENTURE (www.bigmuddyadventure.com). Interactive. Lesson plans and activities for school or home.

CAMP SILOS (www.campsilos.org). Click "Story of Corn," then click "Resources" for primary source material on Chief Black Hawk.

CENTER FOR GLOBAL ENVIRONMENTAL EDUCATION (www.cgee.hamline.edu). K–12 classroom projects and partnership opportunities with the community.

DELTA QUEEN STEAMBOAT COMPANY (www.deltaqueen.com). Descriptions, history, and routes of the company's three boats, one of which is an authentic sternwheeler.

EFFIGY MOUNDS NATIONAL MONUMENT—Effigy Mounds Parks as Classrooms (www.nps.gov/efmo). Virtual tour and graded lesson plans.

ENVIRONMENTAL POLLUTION AGENCY—American Heritage Designated Rivers (www.epa.gov/rivers/98rivers). Click "Upper Mississippi" for information about the state of the river and watershed.

GRAND EXCURSION 2004 (www.grandexcursion.com). Main site for the 2004 reenactment of the 1854 excursion, with education component and many links.

THE HISTORY CHANNEL—The History Channel Classroom Study Guides: The Mighty Mississippi (www.historychannel.com). Guides to each episode in this series, with vocabulary lists and discussion questions.

MISSISSIPPI RIVER PARKWAY COMMISSION (www.mississippiriverinfo.com). Click "Mississippi River Facts" for a list of fun facts.

NATIONAL GEOGRAPHIC SOCIETY— Geography Action! Rivers 2001 (www.nationalgeographic.com/geographyaction). Interactive. Click on "Rivers." Includes printable handout of river vocabulary.

NETSTATE (www.netstate.com). Information about states participating in the 2004 Grand Excursion.

STEAMBOATS.ORG (www.steamboats.org). Interactive. Extensive history, photographs, and river Web cams.

U.S. ARMY CORPS OF ENGINEERS—Rock Island District (www.mvr.usace.army.mil) and St. Paul District (www.mvp.usace.army.mil). Click on "Education Center" for classroom resources and a "Clubhouse" with interactive activities and experiments for kids. Provides downloads of river charts, weather conditions, and environmental reports. Rock Island site links to Henry Peter Bosse's photography, pearl button history, and the interactive "Mississippi River Adventure" hosted by the Memphis District.

U.S. FISH AND WILDLIFE SERVICE (www.fws.gov). Click "Habitat," then "Kids and Educators" for links to interactive educational sites.

USGS WATER SCIENCE FOR SCHOOLS—All about water! (ga.water.usgs.gov/edu). Interactive. Includes pictures, data, and maps.

WATER SKI HALL OF FAME—Milestones (www.waterskihalloffame.com). Timeline of the sport invented on Lake Pepin at Lake City, Minnesota.

WHITE OAK SOCIETY (www.whiteoak.org). Information on fur trading, with links to topics such as living-history sites, museums, crafts, and Native Americans.

CLASSROOM BOOKS

Butler, Dori H. *W Is for Wisconsin.* Black Earth, Wisconsin: Trails Books, 1998.

Costello, Mary C. A. *Climbing the Mississippi River Bridge by Bridge.* Vol. 2. Davenport, Iowa: privately published, 2002.

Eastman, Mary. *Dahcotah, or Life and Legends of the Sioux.* Afton, Minnesota: Afton Historical Society Press, 1995.

Holliday, Diane Young and Malone, Bobbie. *Digging and Discovery: Wisconsin Archaeology.* Madison, Wisconsin: Wisconsin Historical Society, 1997.

Holling, Holling Clancy. *Minn of the Mississippi.* Boston: Houghton Mifflin, 1951.

Lorbiecki, Marybeth. *Painting the Dakota: Seth Eastman at Fort Snelling.* Afton, Minnesota: Afton Historical Society Press, 2000.

Lund, Duane R. *Our Historic Upper Mississippi.* Staples, Minnesota: privately published, 1991.

Malone, Bobbie. *Learning from the Land: Wisconsin Land Use.* Madison, Wisconsin: Wisconsin Historical Society, 1998.

Malone, Bobbie and Gray, Jefferson J. *Working with Water: Wisconsin Waterways.* Madison, Wisconsin: Wisconsin Historical Society, 2001.

Merrick, George B. *Old Times on the Upper Mississippi: The Recollections of a Steamboat Pilot from 1854 to 1863.* Minneapolis: University of Minnesota Press, reprinted 2001. Chicago: Arthur H. Clark, 1909. C. C. Andrews book.

Middleton, Pat. *Mississippi River Activity Guide.* Stoddard, Wisconsin: Heritage Press, 2000.

Middleton, Pat. *America's Great River Road: St. Paul, Minnesota, to Dubuque, Iowa.* Stoddard, Wisconsin: Heritage Press, 2000.

O'Hara, Megan. *Frontier Fort: Fort Life on the Upper Mississippi, 1826.* Mankato, Minnesota: Blue Earth Books, 1998.

Petersen, William J. *Steamboating on the Upper Mississippi.* New York: Dover Publications. Reprinted with alterations 1968. Iowa: State Historical Society of Iowa, 1937.

Shedd, Warner. *The Kids' Wildlife Book.* Charlotte, Vermont: Williamson Publishing Company, 1994.

Smith, Dorothy. *The Log Book of the Sailing Craft "Edith": An 1890 Trip down the Mississippi Made by Three Relatives of Laura Ingalls Wilder.* Privately published, 1984.

Stahl, Dick. *Under the Green Tree Hotel.* Rock Island, Illinois: East Hall Press, 1996.

Titus, Dan. *Tall Tales of the Mississippi River.* Sioux City, Iowa: Quixote Press, 1995.

MORE UPPER MISSISSIPPI BOOKS

Anfinson, John O. *The River We Have Wrought: A History of the Upper Mississippi.* Minneapolis: University of Minnesota Press, 2003.

Burke, William J. *The Upper Mississippi Valley: How the Landscape Shaped our Heritage.* Waukon, Iowa: Mississippi Valley Press, 2000.

Deiss, Ronald. *The Landscape Photographs of Henry Peter Bosse: Upper Mississippi View of the Late Nineteenth Century.* Rock Island, Illinois: U.S. Army Corps of Engineers, Rock Island District, 1998.

Flippo, Kathy. *Between the Saints: Louis and Paul.* Morrison, Missouri: self-published, 1998.

Gillespie, Michael. *Come Hell or High Water: A Lively History of Steamboating on the Mississippi and Ohio Rivers.* Stoddard, Wisconsin: Heritage Press, 2001.

Larson, Ron. *Upper Mississippi River History: Fact-Fiction-Legend.* Winona, Minnesota: Steamboat Press, 1955.

Madson, John. *Up on the River: With the People and Wildlife of the Upper Mississippi.* New York: Lyons Press, 2000.

Malcolm, Andrew H. *Mississippi Currents: Journeys through Time and a Valley.* New York: William Morrow and Company, 1996.

Neuzil, Mark. *Views on the Mississippi: the Photographs of Henry Peter Bosse.* Minneapolis: University of Minnesota Press, 2002.

Twain, Mark. *Life on the Mississippi.* Boston: Osgood and Company, 1883.

Tweet, Roald. *The Quad Cities: An American Mosaic.* Rock Island, Illinois: East Hall Press, 1996.

Way, Frederick Jr. *Way's Packet Directory, 1848–1994.* Athens, Ohio: Ohio University Press, 1983.

GRAND EXCURSION TALES

(and other Mississippi travels of the time)

Andrews, C. C. *Minnesota and Dacotah: in letter descriptive of a tour through the Northwest, in the autumn of 1856.* Washington, D.C.: R. Farnham, 1857. Reprinted as *Minnesota and Dacotah.* New York: Arno Press, 1975.

Dana, Charles A., ed. *The United States, Illustrated.* Vol. 2. New York: Herrmann J. Meyer, 1855.

Hoeffler, Adolf. "Sketches on the Upper Mississippi." *Harper's Monthly Magazine* 7 (June 1853): 177–90.

Lanman, Charles. *A Canoe Voyage up the Mississippi and around Lake Superior in 1846.* New York: D. Appleton and Company, reprinted 1978. Grand Rapids, Michigan: Black Letter Press, 1847.

Petersen, William J. "The Rock Island Railroad Excursion of 1854." *Minnesota History* 15 (Dec. 1934): 405–20.

"Rails West: the Rock Island Excursion of 1854 as Reported by Charles Babcock." *Minnesota History* (Winter 1954): 133–43.

Sedgwick, Catharine. "The Great Excursion to the Falls of St. Anthony." *Putnam's Monthly Magazine* 4 (Sept. 1854): 320–25.

Thorpe, Thomas B. "Remembrances of the Mississippi." *Harper's Monthly Magazine* 12 (Dec. 1855): 25–41.

"The Upper Mississippi." *Harper's Monthly Magazine* 16 (March 1858): 433–54.

"Up the Mississippi." *Emerson's Magazine and Putnam's Monthly* 5 (Oct. 1857): 433–56.

VIDEO

The River Adventure (1988). Dubuque County Historical Society. Order from Mississippi River Museum, P.O. Box 266, Dubuque IA 54004, 319-557-9545.

MUSEUMS AND HISTORIC SITES

This list is restricted to museums and historic sites along the route of the Grand Excursion that feature the river or contain pre–Civil War material. The towns are listed from south to north along the river, from Rock Island, Illinois, to Minneapolis, Minnesota. Local convention and visitors bureaus and chambers of commerce can provide direction to other historic sites. Not included are the countless roadside markers and monuments, scenic overlooks, wildlife preserves, and locks and dams, all of which are worth a stop. Private properties are included only if they have a museum component open to the public.

ROCK ISLAND, ILLINOIS
Colonel Davenport House (1834)
Hauberg Indian Museum / Black Hawk Historic Site
Mississippi River Visitor Center
Rock Island Arsenal Museum
Rock Island Historical Society Home-Museum Complex

DAVENPORT, IOWA
Putnam Museum

LE CLAIRE, IOWA
Buffalo Bill Museum
Cody Homestead
Mississippi Valley Welcome Center

CLINTON, IOWA
Clinton Historical Society Museum
Soaring Eagle Nature Center

BELLEVUE, IOWA
Potter's Mill (1843)
Young Historical Museum

GALENA, ILLINOIS
Dowling House (1826)
Galena Public Library and Historic Collection
Jo Daviess County Museum
Old Market House State Historic Site (1850)
President Ulysses S. Grant Home
Vinegar Hill Historic Leadmine and Museum (1822)
Washburn House State Historic Site (1843, 1860)

DUBUQUE, IOWA
Julien Dubuque Monument (1897)
Mathias Ham House (1833, 1856)
Mississippi River Museum
Mississippi River National Museum and Aquarium (under construction)
Shot Tower (1856)

CASSVILLE, WISCONSIN
Denniston House
Nelson Dewey State Historic Site

GUTTENBERG, IOWA
Lockmaster's House Heritage Museum
State Fish Aquarium and Hatchery

MCGREGOR, IOWA
McGregor Historical Museum

MARQUETTE, IOWA
Marquette Depot Museum

PRAIRIE DU CHIEN, WISCONSIN
B. W. Brisbois House (ca. 1837)
Brisbois Store and Fur Trade Museum (1852)
Joseph Rollette House (1840s) (undergoing
   restoration)
W. H. C. Folsom House (1842)

LANSING, IOWA
Museum of River History

LA CROSSE, WISCONSIN
La Crosse County Historical Society
   Riverside Museum

ONALASKA, WISCONSIN
Upper Mississippi River National Wildlife and
   Fish Refuge Visitors Center

HOMER, MINNESOTA
Willard Bunnell House (mid-1850s)

WINONA, MINNESOTA
Hixon House (1860)
Winona County Historical Society

FOUNTAIN CITY, WISCONSIN
Fountain City Historical Society Museum

ALMA, WISCONSIN
Alma Area Museum

READ'S LANDING, MINNESOTA
Wabasha County Historical Society

WABASHA, MINNESOTA
National Eagle Center

PEPIN, WISCONSIN
Pepin Depot Museum

STOCKHOLM, WISCONSIN
Stockholm Institute and Museum

BAY CITY, WISCONSIN
Pierce County Historical Association River
   Bluffs History Center

RED WING, MINNESOTA
Goodhue County Historical Society

SOUTH ST. PAUL, MINNESOTA
Dakota County Historical Society

COTTAGE GROVE, MINNESOTA
Cottage Grove Area Historical Society

ST. PAUL, MINNESOTA
Historic Fort Snelling (1820s–1830s)
Minnesota Historical Society
Sibley House Historic Site (1838)
Science Museum of Minnesota

MINNEAPOLIS, MINNESOTA
Mill City Museum

Pike's Peak State Park, near McGregor, Iowa
Mount Hosmer Park, Lansing, Iowa
Fish Farm Mounds State Preserve, near
   Marquette, Iowa
Effigy Mounds National Monument, near
   Marquette, Iowa
Black Hawk Park (U.S. Army Corps of
   Engineers), near De Soto, Wisconsin
Pettibone Park, La Crosse, Wisconsin
Perrot State Park, Trempealeau, Wisconsin
Merrick State Park, near Fountain City,
   Wisconsin
Riecks Lake Park, Alma, Wisconsin
Frontenac State Park, Frontenac, Minnesota
Freedom Park, Prescott, Wisconsin
Mercord Mill Park, Prescott, Wisconsin
Indian Mounds Park, St. Paul, Minnesota
Fort Snelling State Park, St. Paul, Minnesota
Minnehaha Park, Minneapolis, Minnesota

RIVER PARKS
(listed south to north)

Le Claire Park, Davenport, Iowa
Illiniwek Forest Preserve, Hampton, Illinois
Riverview Park, Clinton, Iowa
Bellevue State Park, Bellevue, Iowa
Mines of Spain State Park, Dubuque, Iowa
Riverview Park, Dubuque, Iowa
Eagle Point Park, Dubuque, Iowa
Nelson Dewey State Park, Cassville,
   Wisconsin
Wyalusing State Park, Wyalusing, Illinois

Illustration Credits

Effigy Mounds National Monument Museum, Harpers Ferry, Iowa: p. 15, Oneota bowl; p. 72, effigy mounds, sketch by George Catlin.

Fenimore Art Museum, Cooperstown, N.Y.: p. 77, Homer, Minnesota, watercolor by John T. Sperry, 1869.

David Geister: p. 116, The Grand Excursion Arriving in St. Paul, oil sketch by David Geister, 2002.

Hamline University Library, St. Paul, Minnesota: p. 18, The Keel-Boat, engraving from sketch by I.M.L, Harper's Monthly Magazine, December 1855; p. 20, Snags, engraving from sketch by I. M. L, Harper's Monthly Magazine, December 1855; p. 50, The Lead Region—Galena in the Distance, engraving from sketch by J. Dallas, Harper's Monthly Magazine, March 1858; p. 51, Ulysses S. Grant residences before and after the Civil War, engravings from anonymous sketch, Harper's Monthly Magazine, May 1866; p. 106, Lake Pepin, Upper Mississippi, engraving from a drawing by Jacob C. Ward, The Ladies' Repository, 1846; p. 120, Interior of Fort Snelling, engraving from sketch by Adolf Hoeffler, Harper's Monthly Magazine, July 1853.

Isabel Hillman: p. 98, Pepin, Wisconsin, painting by Isabel Hillman.

Historic American Building Survey, Library of Congress, Washington, D.C.: p. 38, Cody House in Le Claire, Iowa, early in the twentieth century.

Illinois State Museum, Springfield: p. 33, Antoine Le Claire, anonymous engraving, ca. 1850.

Paul Clifford Larson photographs: p. 10, sunrise from Pike's Peak, Iowa; p. 23, Lock and Dam 10 at Guttenberg, Iowa; p. 28, 1892 statue of Black Hawk, Hauberg Indian Museum, Rock Island, Illinois; p. 36, early farm machinery at John Deere Pavilion, Moline, Illinois; p. 37, old Bettendorf Axle Factory, Iowa; p. 38, looking past 1851 Old Mill House in Le Claire, Iowa, to Rapid City, Illinois; p. 44, windmill, Fulton, Illinois, and house, Cordova, Illinois; p. 47, Potter's Mill, Bellevue, Iowa; p. 48, causeway to Sabula, Iowa; p. 49, Iowa Boat and Marine machine shop, Bellevue, Iowa; p. 55, Fenelon Place elevator in Dubuque, Iowa; p. 59, looking upriver from Pike's Peak State Park, Iowa; p. 61, Eagle Landmark, steel sculpture by Elmer P. Peterson, La Crosse, Wisconsin; p. 63, Denniston House, Cassville, Wisconsin; p. 66, G. F. Weist's warehouse, built around 1854; p. 67, mussel shells with holes punched for buttons; p. 68, monument to passenger pigeon, Wyalusing State Park, Wisconsin; p. 70, B. W. Brisbois Store of 1851–1852, now Fur Trade Museum, near Prairie du Chien, Wisconsin; p. 73, stilt house, Waukon Junction, Iowa; p. 74, Black Hawk Bridge, Lansing, Iowa; p. 79, 1849 Iowa-Minnesota boundary marker near New Albin, Iowa; p. 80, Lacrosse Players, steel sculpture by Elmer P. Peterson, La Crosse, Wisconsin; p. 83, Trempealeau Mountain viewed from Perot State Park, Wisconsin; p. 85, Willard Bunnell House, Homer, Minnesota; p. 91, relief carving in concrete depicting tundra swans in flight, Winona, Minnesota; p. 92, delta of the Whitewater River filling base of coulee above Kellogg, Minnesota; p. 101, St. Hubert's Lodge, Frontenac, Minnesota; p. 104, house perched above retaining wall, Maiden Rock, Wisconsin; p. 109, modern view of mouth of St. Croix, Prescott, Wisconsin; p. 111, William Le Duc house, Hastings, Minnesota; p. 121, Wabasha Street Bridge, St. Paul, Minnesota.

Library of Congress, Washington, D.C.: p. 65, Partial bird's-eye view of Guttenberg, Iowa, lithograph by Ruger and Stoner, 1869.

Minnesota Historical Society, St. Paul, Minnesota: cover, St. Paul, oil painting by S. Holmes Andrews, 1855; p. 2, Morning Star, 1895; p. 7, Steamboat (Mississippi), oil painting by E. A. Banks, ca. 1870–; p. 14, Indians Spearing Fish 3 Miles below Fort Snelling, watercolor by Seth Eastman, 1846–1848; p. 17, Sioux Encampment, Upper Mississippi, watercolor by F. Jackson, 1857, and Scenery of the Upper Mississippi, An Indian Village, artist unknown, lithograph published by Currier and Ives, circa 1870; p. 19, raft of logs and lumber, 1904; p. 21, woodpile at the foot of Lake Pepin, engraving of an anonymous sketch published by Richardson and Cox, 1847; p. 29, Fort Armstrong, lithograph from painting by Henry Lewis, The Mississippi Valley Illustrated, 1858; p. 32, The War Eagle, ca. 1865; p. 40, Jennie Gilchrist tied up at Green Tree, Iowa, 1880; p. 43, Port Byron, Iowa [actually Illinois], and Berlin, Illinois [actually Iowa], lithograph from painting by Henry Lewis, The Mississippi Valley Illustrated, 1858; p. 49, Redtop on the Mississippi River approaching Dubuque, Iowa, postcard, 1909. p. 52, Dubuque, Iowa, lithograph from painting by Henry Lewis, The Mississippi Valley Illustrated, 1858; p. 69, "Pontoon Bridge and Raft" at Marquette, Iowa, postcard, 1915; p. 71, Fort Crawford in Wisconsin, oil painting by Henry Lewis, 1862; p. 75, The Battle of Bad Axe, lithograph from painting by Henry Lewis, The Mississippi Valley Illustrated, 1858; p. 81, Castle Rock near Winona, cabinet card photograph by Elmer and Tenney, ca. 1870; p. 86, The Soaking Mountain on the Upper Mississippi, engraving from drawing by Jacob C. Ward, The New York Mirror, 1836; p. 88, Winona, oil painting, artist unknown, ca. 1870; p. 90, "Fountain City—Among the Vine-Clad Hills," postcard, 1908; p. 95, Lake Pepin from Chimney Rock, engraving from drawing by E. E. Edwards, 1859, and the American House, Read's Landing, Minnesota, 1870; p. 96, Lake Pepin from Wabasha, oil painting by Clement Haupers, 1949; p. 99, crowd at Lake City, Minnesota, watching Ralph Samuelson water ski behind the WWI Curtis Flying Boat, 1925, and Lake City Ice Yacht Club, 1898, photograph by H. G. Rinkel; p. 102, on the beach at Frontenac, Minnesota, ca. 1880; p. 103, View along the Mississippi River near Maiden Rock, watercolor by Edwin Whitefield, 1856–1859; p. 105, Barn Bluff, Red Wing, Minnesota, watercolor by Edwin Whitefield, 1856–1859, Red Wing, Minnesota, riverfront at base of Barn Bluff, 1860s, and Red Wing, oil painting by Paul Kramer, 1984; p. 107, St. Anthony Falls, oil painting by Ferdinand Richart, 1857; p. 109, The Mouth of the St. Croix River, lithograph from painting by Henry Lewis, The Mississippi Valley Illustrated, 1855; p. 110, We-no-na (first born), photograph by Whitney Gallery, ca. 1865, and Indian woman near Trempealeau, Wisconsin, photograph by Hoard and Tenney, 1875; p. 112, poster promoting city of Nininger, Minnesota; p. 114, Crowd at the Territorial Capitol, anonymous print, 1857; p. 117, Pioneer and Democrat newspaper office, St. Paul, anonymous watercolor, 1858; p. 118, Dakota Indians posing in front of Minnehaha Falls, photograph by Benjamin Upton, 1857; p. 120, Fort Snelling, oil painting by Henry Lewis, 1850.

Muscatine Art Center, Muscatine, Iowa: p. 11, Upper Mississippi River, oil painting by Henry Lewis, 1855; p. 25, Davenport and Rock Island City, oil painting by Henry Lewis, 1855; p. 93, View of the Upper Mississippi, oil painting by Ferdinand Richardt, 1865.

National Mississippi River Museum and Aquarium, Dubuque, Iowa: p. 63, Oneota bowl.

Private collection: p. 16, Black Hawk in Ceremonial Dress, lithograph from a painting by Charles B. King, 1837; p. 22, steamboat dredging at Sabula, Iowa, postcard, ca. 1915; p. 30, U.S. Arsenal shops at Rock Island, Illinois, postcard, 1906; p. 31, Government Bridge of 1872 at Davenport, Iowa, postcard, 1906;

p. 35, Ferry boats between Davenport, Iowa, and Rock Island, Illinois, postcard, ca. 1925; p. 39, Buffalo Bill, postcard, 1952; p. 41, campers on the Mississippi River near Dubuque, Iowa, photographed by Harger and Blish, postcard, 1907; p. 45, log raft arriving at Clinton, Iowa, ca. 1910; p. 46, Lincoln Highway and the new Lyons and Fulton Bridge viewed from Fulton, Illinois, postcard, ca. 1920; p. 47, Lonely Brother Bluff near Savanna, Illinois, postcard, ca. 1930; p. 53, "Tomb of Julien Dubuque, Dubuque, Iowa," postcard, 1907; p. 54, "The Old Deserted Shot Tower, Dubuque, Iowa," postcard, ca. 1930; p. 56, "Steamer J. S. Entering Bridges at Dubuque," postcard, 1911; p. 57, "Wagon and R. R. Bridges Connecting East Dubuque and Dubuque," postcard, 1910; p. 64, Ruins of Nelson Dewey "Castle," near Cassville, Wisconsin, ca. 1920; p. 76, "Bird's Eye View, Genoa, Wis.," postcard, ca. 1905; p. 82, landing and warehouses at La Crosse, Wisconsin, postcard, ca. 1910; p. 84, Trempealeau, Wisconsin, viewed from the south, postcard, ca. 1905; p. 115, St. Paul, lithograph of sketch by J. M. Stanley, 1853; p. 119, "St. Anthony Falls, [Great Northern Railroad Bridge] and Milling District, Minneapolis, Minn.," postcard, ca. 1910.

Smithsonian American Art Museum, Washington, D.C.: p. 9, View on the Upper Mississippi, Beautiful River Bluffs, oil painting by George Catlin, 1835–1836.

Stockholm Institute, Stockholm, Wisconsin: p. 100, trunk belonging to Eric Peterson, first settler of Stockholm, Wisconsin.

U.S. Army Corps of Engineers, Rock Island District Archives: p. 86, Queen's Bluff, photograph by Henry Bosse, 1885; p. 113, Pine Bend, wing dams below St. Paul, Minnesota, photograph by Henry Bosse, 1891.

U.S. Army Corps of Engineers, St. Paul District Archives: p. 74, De Soto, Wisconsin, photograph by Henry Bosse, 1891.

University of Minnesota Libraries, Minneapolis, Minnesota: p. 8, Traveller's Guide through the United States and Canada by Wellington Williams, 1851; p. 13, Bluffs below St. Paul, engraving by Herrmann J. Meyer, The United States Illustrated, 1853–1855; p. 27, Rock Island City, engraving by Herrmann J. Meyer, The United States Illustrated, 1853–1855; p. 58, Eagle Point, near Dubuque, engraving from sketch by Alfred R. Waud, Picturesque America, 1872; p. 61, Buena Vista, a steep bluff between Dubuque and Guttenberg, Iowa, engraving from sketch by Alfred R. Waud, Picturesque America, 1872; p. 87, detail of J. H. Colton's map of Minnesota Territory, 1856; p. 97, detail of J. H. Colton's map of Minnesota Territory, 1856.

Winona County Historical Society, Winona, Minnesota: p. 12, Woodland culture mound builders; p. 24, Sunday Afternoon on the Levee in Winona, Minnesota, oil painting by S. J. Durran, 1895; p. 89, plat map of Rolling Stone, Minnesota; p. 119, St. Anthony Falls, engraving by Herrmann J. Meyer, ca. 1853.

Wisconsin Historical Society, Madison, Wisconsin: p. 62, inside a lead mine near Cassville, Wisconsin, ca. 1900 (image no. WHi-2214); p. 71, View of the Great Treaty Held at Prairie du Chien, September 1825, engraving from painting by J. O. Lewis, 1835 (image no. Whi-3242).